Saving the Wo. ___ *..r War*

Johns Hopkins Nuclear History and Contemporary Affairs
Martin J. Sherwin, Series Editor

Saving the World from Nuclear War

The June 12, 1982, Disarmament Rally and Beyond

VINCENT J. INTONDI

Johns Hopkins University Press
Baltimore

© 2023 Johns Hopkins University Press
All rights reserved. Published 2023
Printed in the United States of America on acid-free paper

2 4 6 8 9 7 5 3 1

Johns Hopkins University Press
2715 North Charles Street
Baltimore, Maryland 21218
www.press.jhu.edu

Library of Congress Cataloging-in-Publication Data

Names: Intondi, Vincent J., author.
Title: Saving the world from nuclear war : The June 12, 1982, disarmament
    rally and beyond / Vincent Intondi.
Description: Baltimore, Maryland : Johns Hopkins University Press, 2023. |
    Series: Johns Hopkins nuclear history and contemporary affairs |
    Includes bibliographical references and index.
Identifiers: LCCN 2022033567 | ISBN 9781421446400 (paperback) |
    ISBN 9781421446417 (ebook)
Subjects: LCSH: Antinuclear movement—New York (State)—
    New York—History—20th century. | Nuclear disarmament—History—
    20th century. | United Nations. General Assembly. Special Session on
    Disarmament (2nd : 1982) | BISAC: HISTORY / Modern / 20th Century /
    General | POLITICAL SCIENCE / Political Process / Political Advocacy
Classification: LCC JZ5584.U6 I67 2023 | DDC 303.6/6—dc23/eng/20221110
LC record available at https://lccn.loc.gov/2022033567

A catalog record for this book is available from the British Library.

The photograph on page 81 is used courtesy of Seymour Chwast. All other
images are courtesy of the Dorothy Marder Collection, 1971–1999 (DG
233), Series B, Box 19, in the Swarthmore College Peace Collection.

*Special discounts are available for bulk purchases of this book. For more
information, please contact Special Sales at specialsales@jh.edu.*

*For Marty, Natalie, and all those who fight
for a world without nuclear weapons*

CONTENTS

AAEC	African-American Executive Committee
ABM	anti-ballistic missile
ACDA	Arms Control and Disarmament Agency
AFDC	Aid to Families with Dependent Children
AFL-CIO	American Federation of Labor and Congress of Industrial Organizations
AFSC	American Friends Service Committee
ASCF	American Security Council Foundation
AUP	Athletes United for Peace
BAN	Blacks Against Nukes
BUF	Black United Front
CALC	Clergy and Laity Concerned
CBC	Congressional Black Caucus
CETA	Comprehensive Employment and Training Act
CLW	Council for a Livable World
CND	Campaign for Nuclear Disarmament
FANTF	Feminist Anti-Nuclear Task Force
FAS	Federation of American Scientists
FEMA	Federal Emergency Management Agency
FOR	Fellowship of Reconciliation
GCN	Gay Community News
ICAN	International Campaign to Abolish Nuclear Weapons
ICBM	intercontinental ballistic missile
INF	Intermediate-Range Nuclear Forces
IPPNW	International Physicians for the Prevention of Nuclear War
JCPOA	Joint Comprehensive Plan of Action

MFS	Mobilization for Survival
MOBE	National Mobilization Committee
MTV	Music Television
NAARPR	National Alliance Against Racist and Political Oppression
NOAR	National Organization for an American Revolution
NPR	Nuclear Posture Review
NWFC	Nuclear Weapons Freeze Campaign
NWFTF	Nuclear Weapons Facilities Task Force
PAND	Performing Artists for Nuclear Disarmament
PSR	Physicians for Social Responsibility
SALT	Strategic Arms Limitation Treaty
SANE	Committee for a Sane Nuclear Policy
SDI	Strategic Defense Initiative
SHAD	Sound-Hudson Against Atomic Development
SNCC	Student Nonviolent Coordinating Committee
SSD	Special Session on Disarmament
SSDII	Second Special Session on Disarmament
START	Strategic Arms Reduction Treaty
TMI	Three Mile Island
TPNW	Treaty on the Prohibition of Nuclear Weapons
TWPPC	Third World and Progressive People's Coalition
UCS	Union of Concerned Scientists
UN	United Nations
WAND	Women's Action for Nuclear Disarmament
WCAPS	Women of Color Advancing Peace, Security, and Conflict Transformation
WILPF	Women's International League for Peace and Freedom
WPS	Women's Party for Survival
WRL	War Resisters League

The sun was shining without a cloud in the sky. Cars and bicycles were weaving in and out as traffic filled the streets of Manhattan. Tourists taking selfies seemed to appear on every block as people rushed through the streets, many on their way to work. I decided to arrive early, walk around Central Park, and take it all in. For me, it never got old: the music, food, and conversations. I still loved how you could get lost and forget, for at least a moment, that you were inside the city that never sleeps. It was three years before we would ever hear of COVID-19.

As I walked around Central Park, I eventually made my way to the Great Lawn. I could not help but stare at the green grass, thinking about what had transpired almost forty years ago. Here I was, standing in the same place where a million others had rallied to save the world from nuclear war. I sat thinking about what it must have been like to hear Bruce Springsteen, Jackson Browne, and Rita Marley belt out lyrics so that future generations could one day live without the fear of nuclear war. I thought of what it must have felt like for the *hibakusha* (atomic bomb survivors) to travel to the very country that dropped the atomic bombs on Hiroshima and Nagasaki and join American citizens in saying, "Never Again!" I tried to imagine the poets who were on street corners around Central Park reciting words of peace while New York City police officers maintained order with a smile. I tried to imagine what it must have felt like to be part of something that historic. At that moment, I heard a familiar voice. I looked over, and there sat Leslie Cagan, who said, "Hello. Why don't we just talk here." I agreed and added, "Let's start from the beginning."

PART I

SETTING THE STAGE

CHAPTER I

Introduction

Sleep had become a foreign concept. Food was an afterthought. Volunteers' fingers were sore and calloused from hours of typing and dialing telephones. It was 2:00 a.m. on June 12, 1982. Working on a mix of adrenaline, coffee, and a deep commitment to halting the nuclear arms race, organizers finalized last-minute details, including the order of speakers and instructions for the hundreds of medical and legal personnel who were going to be on standby throughout the day. Many suspected the rally would be big based on the number of buses and trains that had already arrived. No one knew how big. Late into the night, workers were busy erecting the massive stage in Central Park. "Nobody ever asks about stages," one worker said. "It's forty feet by sixty feet. We have sound wings that are sixteen feet by thirty feet with sound towers forty-six feet high on each side. Speakers are hanging by five-ton motors. When we finish, the stage will be as tall as a five-story building."[1]

Later that day, atomic bomb survivors (*hibakusha*) joined one million people from around the world in saying, "No More Hiroshimas," in what would become the largest antinuclear demonstration in history and the largest rally of any kind to take place in the United States. When asked why they drove ten hours from Ottawa to attend, one couple responded: "Because we choose life." Another man said he and so many others were in Central Park because, "We want to save the world." "There's no way the leaders can ignore us now," declared Alex Willentz, who had driven overnight from Utica, New York. "It's not just hippies and crazies anymore. It's everybody." Willentz was not exaggerating. People came to New York from every corner of the country and, indeed, the world to demand an end to the nuclear arms race.[2]

Organizers called the June 12, 1982, demonstration "the disarmament rally to end all disarmament rallies."[3] The purpose of the march was to show support for the United Nations Second Special Session on Disarmament and to call for a reduction of all nuclear weapons and a transfer of military budgets to human needs.[4] This historic event was the height of a movement that began when the United States dropped the first atomic bombs on Hiroshima and Nagasaki in 1945, and that movement is once again trying to find its voice in the twenty-first century.

This rally was unlike any other in American history. The sheer size of the demonstration was unmatched at the time. June 12 dwarfed previous protests in the country, including those that were in opposition to the Vietnam War. Since then, June 12 has become part of a larger legacy of citizen mobilization that has led to more recent events like the worldwide Women's March in 2017, which occurred in response to Donald J. Trump's presidential election. The one million people who gathered in Central Park proved that the antinuclear movement was more intersectional and diverse than previously thought, contributed to the Reagan administration changing course on nuclear weapons, and paved the way for a new generation of activists committed to saving the world from nuclear annihilation.

For many people, the fear that President Ronald Reagan would start a nuclear war and the hope they received from attending the June 12 rally were what inspired them to take up the antinuclear banner. When Donald Trump became president of the United States in 2016, I began to witness a growing fear and heightened awareness of nuclear weapons not shown since the 1980s. The hope, however, was missing. I began to write this book.

Throughout President Trump's tenure, the world witnessed his impulsive and cavalier attitude about nuclear weapons. When discussing nuclear weapons, Trump stated he would not only "bomb the shit out of terrorists" but also kill "their family members."[5] He withdrew from the 2015 Joint Comprehensive Plan of Action, commonly referred to as the "Iran nuclear deal," despite the fact it was working to constrain

Iran's potential to make a bomb. On December 22, 2016, Trump said, "The United States must greatly strengthen and expand its nuclear capability until such time as the world comes to its senses regarding nukes." When questioned the following day, he doubled down, boasting, "Let it be an arms race." When North Korea announced in 2017 that it was getting close to testing an intercontinental ballistic missile (ICBM), Trump—rather than exploring the possibility of diplomacy—simply tweeted, "It won't happen," and suggested that South Korea and Japan develop their own nuclear weapons in response. North Korea later flight-tested the missile, which prompted Trump to threaten "fire and fury." In his 2018 Nuclear Posture Review, Trump proposed new low-yield nuclear warheads, a new sea-launched cruise missile, and a delay in retiring the last megaton-class gravity bomb. His review also contained new language that made clear the United States would consider use of nuclear weapons in response to a "non-nuclear strategic attack." Trump officials explored the idea of breaking the global moratorium on nuclear testing and, in May 2020, Trump's "arm control" envoy said that the United States is prepared to spend Russia and China "into oblivion" in order to win a new nuclear arms race.[6]

With heightened awareness of all things nuclear, a new movement emerged, led primarily by women and younger activists, who viewed eliminating racism, patriarchy, and nuclear weapons as part of the same fight to create a more just and equal world. Even when Trump was in office, however, there was nowhere near the level of action from the American public that had occurred in the 1980s. We must ask ourselves, why? To answer this question, it is crucial to look back at when another president, Ronald Reagan, repeatedly employed dangerous rhetoric when discussing nuclear weapons and how the world responded.

Typically, discussions that focus on antinuclear activities of the 1980s are reduced to the nuclear freeze campaign, and for good cause. Rarely have we seen a democratic, citizen-led movement of this magnitude in the United States. Historians have examined the success of the freeze campaign on the local, state, and federal levels, along with its ability to appeal to the masses. The June 12 rally is usually viewed as one event in the overall freeze movement. The rally, however, was not a freeze event, and the antinuclear movement as a whole in the 1980s included much more than the freeze campaign. Therefore, while this is not the first book to examine the antinuclear movement of the 1980s, my intent is to focus specifically on the June 12 rally, those who made it happen, and how it fits into the larger issues of peace and intersectionality.

As Henry Maar III argues, much of the scholarship on this topic takes a top-down approach, focusing on the actions of President Reagan and general secretary of the Soviet Union Mikhail Gorbachev, in ending the Cold War and changing their views on nuclear weapons. Putting government leaders at the center of the narrative ignores the power of organizers, activists, and ordinary citizens who worked tirelessly to halt the nuclear arms race.[7] For those like Helen Caldicott, Leslie Cagan, David Cortright, Randy Kehler, and others whom I interviewed for this book, the concern was about an entire system that threatened the end of civilization. Many grew up with the Cuban Missile Crisis and Vietnam War, often having to practice duck and cover drills in school. For these activists and millions around the world, the fear of nuclear war was real and the time to act was now.

People of various races, faiths, ideologies, and sexual orientations were present on June 12, each with their own reason for attending. For some, ending the nuclear arms race was linked to their religious faith. Others, especially those in the Black community, saw a direct link between the amount of money being spent on nuclear weapons and eliminating badly needed social programs that benefitted the poor. Many viewed nuclear weapons as part of the overall military industrial complex, which included US intervention in Central America and the Middle East. Some even arrived just to see a free concert and then became educated to the cause, while others attended the rally out of a genuine fear the that the United States and Soviet Union would start a nuclear war.

Although the antinuclear movement is often described as a single-issue campaign, unrelated to race or gender and dominated by white, middle-class supporters, this was not the case. People of color, women, and the LGBTQ community have fought for nuclear disarmament since 1945, and they were integral in the movement to end the arms race throughout the 1980s. Examining the June 12 rally and its diversity shows how civil rights, LGBTQ, and feminist agitation did not slow down in the 1980s. They just switched lanes to the vital issue of nuclear war. Indeed, Black, gay, and female activists were among those who led the organizing efforts for the June 12 rally. They showed that nuclear weapons affected everyone. In this regard, June 12 serves as a microcosm for the antinuclear movement. If one were to view aerial photos of the crowd in Central Park that day, it would appear to validate the notion that only white, middle-class people supported nuclear disarmament. However, the view on the ground painted a much different picture. Led by the Reverend Herbert Daughtry and the Black United Front, African Americans comprised 50 percent of the leadership that day. Prominent Native Americans spoke. Rita Marley, Richie Havens, and Chaka Khan performed, and Coretta Scott King, Ossie Davis, and Ruby Dee addressed the crowd. Thousands poured into Central Park from Harlem, Brooklyn, and other parts of New York, while delegations from around the world marched and rallied to halt the arms race.

Recently, we have seen a reexamination of the antinuclear movement that looks beyond the normal cast of characters. Scholars are studying the antinuclear movement through the lens of race, gender, and class. Marginalized groups, including African Americans, the LGBTQ community, and women, have all begun to get their due, and in doing so, they have altered the way we view the antinuclear movement as a monolith.[8] Examining the June 12 rally builds on this narrative and attempts to debunk the idea that only white men led this movement.

Immediately following the atomic bombings of Hiroshima and Nagasaki, the movement to abolish nuclear weapons began. Members of the scientific, religious, and African American communities criticized President Harry Truman's decision to use nuclear weapons in Japan, with many calling for nuclear disarmament before any organized movement formed. Following World War II, the Cold War and the nuclear arms race began. As the number of nuclear weapons around the world increased, so too did the voices saying, "No More Hiroshimas." New organizations formed, and individuals dedicated themselves to the cause of nuclear disarmament. However, as the movement pushed forward, it often seemed to run into a brick wall, halting momentum. With Congress reconstituting the House Un-American Activities Committee (HUAC) and the rise of McCarthyism in the 1950s, to be antinuclear was synonymous with being pro-communism. Various organizations and individuals were silenced, especially in the Black community. A decade later, the antinuclear movement once again pushed forward with the rise of groups like Committee for a Sane Nuclear Policy (SANE) and Women Strike for Peace (WSP). The 1962 Cuban Missile Crisis reminded the world how close we were to ending life on the planet. A year later, President John F. Kennedy signed the Nuclear Test Ban Treaty. While it appeared that the nuclear issue would remain front and center, the movement struggled to stay relevant throughout the 1960s with the civil rights movement hitting its stride and the start of the Vietnam War.

By the end of the 1970s, much had changed in the United States. The Federal Bureau of Investigation (FBI) and its Counterintelligence Program (COINTELPRO), under the direction of J. Edgar Hoover, had successfully neutralized many of the most influential and powerful voices for peace and freedom in the United States. The civil rights, Black Power, and women's liberation movements appeared to have peaked. The Vietnam War was over and so too was the antiwar movement. Many veterans of the war and activists from these various movements suffered from post-traumatic stress disorder (PTSD). Others were serving time in prison. Some chose to flee the United States or were forced underground to avoid imprisonment or worse. "You could hardly find the peace movement," David Cortright said. "Once the United States had withdrawn from Indochina, there was little or nothing going on in the peace community."[9]

At the same time, the Right was positioning itself for a resurgence after the defeat of Barry Goldwater in 1964 and the embarrassment of Richard Nixon a decade later. As protests filled the streets, the Republican Party began to develop new strategies to target voters with the emergence of a bevy of right-wing think tanks, further aligning itself with the evangelical community and fully embracing the "Southern Strategy." Many voters wanted a president who would kick the "Vietnam Syndrome." Coupled with unrest in the Middle East, a stalling economy, and President Jimmy Carter having to fight off a primary challenge from Senator Ted Kennedy (D-MA), a perfect storm was created, and in November 1980, Ronald Reagan became the 40th president of the United States.

While Reagan's victory provided conservatives with a reason to celebrate, it also awoke a sleeping giant. The antinuclear movement, which had been struggling to find its voice during the Vietnam War, reemerged. Established groups like SANE, the Union of Concerned Scientists, and Physicians for Social Responsibility expanded their membership. New groups like Performing Artists for Nuclear Disarmament (PAND), Dancers for Disarmament, and Athletes United for Peace formed. Seasoned activists Randy Kehler, David Cortright, David McReynolds, Cora Weiss, Leslie Cagan, and Herbert Daughtry, as well as newcomers like Randall Forsberg and Kathy Engel, committed themselves to stopping the nuclear arms race.

To alter the Reagan administration's nuclear policies, organizers knew the key was to change how the larger public viewed nuclear weapons. They would need an army of activists and concerned citizens to fight the forces who called for a winnable nuclear war. They would need a million people in the streets demanding nuclear disarmament.

For this demonstration to be successful, organizers also knew they would need a clear message. Much like the freeze campaign, June 12 needed a simple, yet effective slogan that would resonate with people throughout the country. The rally would have to transcend race, gender, class, and religion. It would have to unite folks from across the political aisle. Activists would have to educate the public about the true dangers of nuclear war in a way few had done before. They would need allies at every level of government to champion their cause. They would need celebrities to spread the message and help raise the necessary funds to pull off something of this magnitude. They would need the voices of the *hibakusha*. Who or what could bring all them together? In a word: Reagan.

President Reagan proved to the be the catalyst activists needed. Reagan ushered in a new era in defense spending and employed rhetoric that made clear that using nuclear weapons was a real possibility. As a result, the antinuclear movement in the 1980s became one the largest social movements in United States history. As Paul Rubinson points out, "These women and men wrote books, marched, broke laws, petitioned Congress, sued, sang, spoke, and even exercised in opposition to nuclear weapons."[10] Rubinson correctly argues that diversity gave the antinuclear movement its strength. However, historians have offered a different perspective, arguing that the movement was less effective because of its inclusiveness. Some contend that the divide between activists who were motivated by idealism and those who were more pragmatic in their approach stymied the movement. Rubinson mentions that "some activists wanted arms control, while others demanded disarmament. A number of women felt marginalized within the movement, and some African Americans felt patronized by white organizers. Opponents of nuclear power did not automatically protest nuclear weapons. Americans rose up against missile systems near their homes, but not those located elsewhere."[11] All of these factors provided a challenge for the organizers of June 12, making it even more remarkable that they were able to pull off a rally and march of this size.

This book begins with the election of Ronald Reagan as president of the United States. Immediately upon taking office, President Reagan announced plans for the largest military buildup in history. Coupled with the rhetoric coming out of the administration about a "winnable nuclear war" and bellicose statements regarding the Soviet Union, the antinuclear movement, which had been largely dormant since the Vietnam War, awakened. In addition to the Reagan administration, nuclear power accidents like Three Mile Island and the influence of Cold War culture, including numerous books and films, all contributed to the reemergence of the antinuclear movement. This movement combined old voices as well as new. Groups began to see the connections between race, gender, and nuclear weapons. This chapter also introduces some of the leading individuals and organizations that featured prominently in the June 12, 1982, demonstration and sets the stage for the most important protest in United States history.

In the winter of 1981, veteran peace activists David Cortright, David McReynolds, Cora Weiss, and Mike Myerson were discussing the upcoming United Nations Second Special Session on Disarmament and decided they should plan something big for the event. Out of this conversation came the June 12 rally. Chapter 3 examines the enormous planning of the rally while focusing on interviews with the main organizers and leaders of the rally committee. Analyzing the planning stages shows the number of diverse voices who made this day possible, but also illustrates the problems that arose, including how organizers avoided a near collapse of the entire rally.

After almost a year of organizing, the day arrived. From the early morning hours to when the last person left Central Park, chapter 4 explores the "disarmament rally to end all disarmament rallies." In addition to speeches and events happening on stage, this chapter discusses the attitudes of rank-and-file participants and the experience of the day through the eyes of the main organizers.

I have never been one to study history if only to leave it in the past. Therefore, this book concludes by analyzing the legacy of June 12. What do the organizers think today about the 1980s? Were they successful? Did this rally affect the attitudes of the Reagan administration? Would they have done things differently? Could June 12 ever be replicated? Looking at June 12 forces us to examine whether protests, public pressure, and organizing work to change policy. Does organizing around fear work? This chapter also examines the current movement to eliminate nuclear weapons, including the Nobel Peace Prize–winning International Campaign to Abolish Nuclear Weapons (ICAN), asking, where do we go from here to ensure future generations will live in a world free of nuclear weapons?

It was Sunday afternoon on a beautiful autumn day in Washington, DC. While not as warm as it was in June 1982, the sun was certainly shining. I was in my office doing research for this book when I stopped momentarily to reflect on what was happening in the next room over. Beyond the Bomb, the nuclear disarmament organization led by a group of incredibly talented women, was conducting its "Bomb Squad Lab" training. About twenty-five students from around the country were learning how to lobby, write effective letters to the editor, organize campaigns, and use digital formats as activists. I thought about how this diverse group of students were one room over expressing hope, courage, and confidence that they were going to change the world, as photos of Malcolm X, Angela Davis, Sojourner Truth, and Paul Robeson stared back at them from the walls. I had spoken to the group the day before on the history of Black antinuclear activism. And then it happened. I was reading a speech by Jack O'Dell when I received a notification that he had just died. For me, this book instantly became more important. I felt an obligation to ensure it was completed.

Much has been written about Jack O'Dell's work in the Black freedom struggle, but his role in the antinuclear movement is still largely ignored. O'Dell was a fixture in the civil rights movement. Born Hunter Pitts O'Dell, "Jack" was an organizer and advisor to Dr. Martin Luther King Jr. O'Dell ran King's Southern Christian Leadership Conference in Harlem and the Voter Education Project in Atlanta. He regularly wrote for *Freedomways*, the quarterly founded by W. E. B. Du Bois, often highlighting the work of groups like the Student Nonviolent Coordinating Committee and explaining to readers the connections between capitalism, racism, and imperialism. O'Dell counseled King on his opposition to the Vietnam War and years later joined the Reverend Jesse Jackson working with Operation PUSH (People United to Save Humanity) and the Rainbow Coalition. However, throughout all of his work in the Black freedom movement, O'Dell was active in the fight for nuclear disarmament and often acted as a bridge between the two movements.[12] He was a committed antinuclear activist and deserves credit for what he, along with so many others, was able to accomplish in the 1980s. My hope in writing this book is that readers can learn from those like O'Dell who came before us, helped change the course of history, and saved the world from nuclear war.

While I have interviewed many of those who were on the front lines organizing the march and rally, undoubtedly, I am leaving voices out. Some have passed on. For others, memories have faded. Although they may not be mentioned by name, they are not forgotten. Nor are the hundreds of thousands of people who attended the rally, returned home, and continued to fight for nuclear disarmament, ensuring that June 12, 1982, was not a moment, but part of a movement that will continue until the world is finally free of nuclear weapons.

CHAPTER 2

The Movement Awakens

In 1979, a 38-year-old woman rented a cramped, small room on Harvard Street in Brookline, Massachusetts. Here, in what became her office, the woman thought about how she and the world had gotten to this point. Born in Alabama, the little-known defense analyst was raised in New York and graduated from Barnard College with a degree in English. After teaching in Bryn Mawr, Pennsylvania, Randall Forsberg moved to Stockholm in the late 1960s. There she began a new job as a typist for the Stockholm International Peace Research Institute, a think tank the Swedish government established in 1966 to monitor the arms race worldwide. In Sweden, as she began to read the reports about the nuclear arms race, the veil was lifted. She knew she could not ignore what she was reading. Two decades had passed since the atomic bombings of Hiroshima and Nagasaki, and the world seemed closer than ever to nuclear war. The United States and the Soviet Union appeared to have no intention of slowing down as the number of countries joining the nuclear club steadily increased. To Forsberg, it was not a matter of if, but when there would be a global Hiroshima.[1]

When Forsberg returned to the United States, she enrolled at the Massachusetts Institute of Technology, determined to find a way to apply her scholarly abilities to the cause of peace. She set out to create a series of proposals that could unite traditional peace groups with ordinary citizens in a common campaign for ending the arms race.[2] As a result, Forsberg created a "Call to Halt the Arms Race," or the nuclear freeze proposal. She was convinced that the antinuclear movement would be far more effective if organizations united behind a proposal for a US-Soviet agreement to halt the testing, production, and deployment of nuclear weapons.[3] Her proposal would become a manifesto for peace the likes of which the United States had never seen.

Throughout the early 1970s, nuclear disarmament did not garner the attention it once did in the 1940s and '50s. Most peace groups and arms control advocates were focused solely on ending the Vietnam War. Moreover, for many who were dedicated to the nuclear issue, it appeared their work had paid off. The Nuclear Non-Proliferation Treaty of 1968 and the Strategic Arms Limitation Treaty (SALT I) in 1972, combined with Soviet-American détente and various arms control negotiations, made it seem as though the chances of nuclear war were diminishing. On the basis of these developments, the United Nations went so far as to label the 1970s the "Disarmament Decade."[4] Therefore, groups like SANE, Women's International League for Peace and Freedom (WILPF), and Women Strike for Peace (WSP) that had been fighting for nuclear disarmament were at low points in membership and support.

Despite all of the treaties and agreements, the development of nuclear weapons actually increased in the 1970s. France rejected the partial test ban treaty and, along with China, Israel, India, and South Africa, refused to sign the Nuclear Non-Proliferation Treaty. Moreover, the various treaties between the United States and the Soviet Union focused more on negotiating a way to keep nuclear weapons rather than eliminate them. Nuclear arms controls and détente were beginning to lose their appeal. As a result, between 1972 and 1977, the US government added 4,500 strategic nuclear warheads and bombs, bringing the total to about 9,000. The Soviet Union increased its strategic arsenal from some 2,500 to 3,650, and an estimated ten nations moved closer to becoming nuclear powers. The Soviet Union deployed a new generation of intermediate-range nuclear missiles, the SS-20s. These missiles could target Western Europe for nuclear destruction far more effectively than ever before. In response, President Carter moved forward with his plan to develop a new nuclear weapon: the neutron bomb. Slated for deployment in Western Europe, the neutron bomb relied on radiation rather than heat and blast to kill people. None of the nuclear powers seemed willing to explore the possibility of total disarmament, and nuclear fears began to rise. As a result, antinuclear organizations grew substantially in Western Europe, North America, and the Pacific in the mid-1970s, and by 1978, a global campaign against nuclear weapons had reemerged, laying the groundwork for the full awakening in the 1980s.[5]

In 1976, the War Resisters League (WRL) took the lead in organizing the Continental Walk for Nuclear Disarmament and Social Justice, in which "the case for disarmament was taken to the people, town by town." Organizers called for the United States to unilaterally begin the process of ending the arms race, reduce military spending, and shift its focus to rebuilding inner cities. The plan was to unite African Americans, groups representing the global south, the LGBTQ community, women's groups, and organized labor by having citizens join together in a 3,600-mile walk around the country, converging in Washington, DC.[6]

The following summer, the WRL national committee voted to make "disarmament and peace conversion" the highest priority for the next year. Lawrence Wittner, who has written extensively on the nuclear disarmament movement, mentions that "In September 1978, WRL members staged simultaneous demonstrations in Red Square and on the White House lawn, where they unfurled banners calling upon the two Cold War antagonists to disarm. Similarly, in early 1978 the Fellowship of Reconciliation (FOR) national council voted to reaffirm disarmament as their major priority. The group's magazine, *Fellowship*, explained: 'Our membership and leadership agreed that, in view of the accelerating arms race between the U.S. and USSR and their client states, other programmatic concerns must, for the moment, take second place.'"[7]

Following the end of the Vietnam War, the American Friends Service Committee (AFSC) shifted its focus once again to nuclear disarmament. The group stepped up its support for a nationwide campaign against the B-1 bomber, a nuclear-capable weapons system. It also expanded local organizing efforts that were beginning to take hold. Women Strike for Peace, which was instrumental in pushing for a nuclear test ban treaty, assailed the neutron bomb and distributed a brochure titled "Human Beings Are an Endangered Species." It also petitioned President Carter to enter into negotiations to end the arms race.

Clergy and Laity Concerned went all in on stopping the B-1 bomber and nuclear weapons making facilities.[8]

Antinuclear activism also began to resonate in the US scientific community, including the Federation of American Scientists (FAS) and the Union of Concerned Scientists (UCS). In 1978, UCS issued a "Declaration on the Nuclear Arms Race." Signed by thousands of scientists, the statement called for US initiatives to halt the production of nuclear weapons. The *Bulletin of the Atomic Scientists* suggested that the US government simply "stop the race in accumulation of new weapons and weapon delivery systems" on a temporary basis, to see if the Soviet Union would follow.[9]

US peace groups worked together on the 1978 UN Special Session on Disarmament (SSD). In 1961, the nonaligned nations had proposed that the United Nations hold a special session dedicated to nuclear disarmament. Over fifteen years passed before these nations again proposed the idea in the form of a World Disarmament Conference. However, when plans collapsed in 1976, the major powers reluctantly agreed to hold the special session on disarmament. The resolution for the special session thus passed unanimously in the General Assembly, and in May 1978, the United Nations, for the first time, met to discuss a program dedicated to universal disarmament. Recognizing the special session's potential for mobilizing public opinion and changing public policy, US and overseas disarmament groups promoted public awareness of the event, met together frequently, issued disarmament proposals, lobbied government officials, and even hosted seminars on disarmament for the official UN delegations from small nations. On May 27, they staged a march through Manhattan and a rally for nuclear disarmament outside the United Nations buildings, which drew an estimated fifteen to twenty thousand people—probably the largest disarmament demonstration at that point in US history. Although the UN special session did not lead to a breakthrough in the realm of public policy, it secured an agreement by the United Nations that the arms race jeopardized the security of all nations, substantially enhanced the role of disarmament NGOs in UN affairs, focused the energies of disparate groups, and raised public consciousness. Furthermore, from the standpoint of peace groups, the UN special session produced an excellent

"Final Document"—the result, in part, of their lobbying, which they championed thereafter.[10]

William Knoblauch argues that in addition to the fear of nuclear war, other factors contributed to the heightened awareness about all things nuclear. In March 1979, there was the reactor accident at Pennsylvania's Three Mile Island. Two weeks later, the film *The China Syndrome*, which depicted an eerily similar chain of events, was released. Then in July, a massive uranium spill near Church Rock, New Mexico, contaminated the nearby Puerco River.[11]

Moreover, Knoblauch mentions various geopolitical events of 1979 that also contributed to the rise of nuclear fear, including the Iranian Revolution, which, led to the overthrow of Mohammad Reza Shah Pahlavi and the installation of the radical Shiʻa cleric Ayatollah Ruhollah Khomeini. In December, the Soviet Union invaded Afghanistan, prompting President Carter to halt technological exchanges with the Soviets, withdraw the US Olympic team from the 1980 summer games in Moscow, and remove the second Strategic Arms Limitation Treaty (SALT II) from Senate consideration. Carter called the Soviet invasion the greatest threat to world peace since World War II and proclaimed in his "Carter Doctrine" that any Soviet attempt to control the oil-rich Persian Gulf region would be considered a threat to vital US interests. As the 1970s came to a close, the Cold War seemed to be heating up. All of these developments, coupled with the end of the Vietnam War and the first UN Special Session on Disarmament in 1978, began to awaken the antinuclear movement. The full mobilization, however, came a year later.[12]

When Ronald Reagan was elected president, the prospects for arms control appeared dismal. As David Meyer argues in *A Winter of Discontent*, the election of Ronald Reagan made things "worse and appear much worse." Candidate Reagan attacked Carter's weakness in standing up to the Soviet Union, likening arms control to appeasement. If Carter's campaign rhetoric appeared hawkish, Reagan's was on another level. Reagan interpreted his landslide victory as a "broad mandate of support for his foreign and domestic policies, among them opposition to arms control," Meyer writes.[13] Douglas Waller contends that "never before had a modern American president entered office so publicly opposed to arms control." Reagan flirted with the idea of a preemptive first strike and ventured that nuclear war could be survivable. He promised a "housecleaning" of arms control advocates in the State Department. He pledged to accelerate an arms race to make the US military superior to the Soviet Union's and to "bring the Russian bear to its knees at the negotiating table." Reagan falsely asserted that the United States had unilaterally disarmed in the 1970s and that submarine-launched ballistic missiles were recallable. The new president dismissed nuclear nonproliferation, and when asked if he wanted the nation to return to the days of the Cold War, he replied, "When did the Cold War ever end?" As *Time* magazine editor Strobe Talbott observed, "Reagan and his administration came into office not really wanting to pursue arms control at all."[14]

The president and his advisers believed that the United States had been weakened militarily by arms control treaties. The administration's view toward arms control was epitomized by Pentagon official Richard Perle to Richard Starr in 1983. Commenting on the deadlocked conventional arms talks in Vienna, which had languished for fifteen years without agreement, Perle said: "Congratulations! You obviously did a good job because nothing happened."[15] Indeed, Reagan never met an arms control agreement he could support. Reagan opposed the 1963 Partial Test Ban Treaty, signed by President John F. Kennedy, which banned aboveground nuclear testing. He opposed the 1968 Nuclear Non-Proliferation Treaty, signed by President Lyndon B. Johnson, which attempted to halt the spread of nuclear weapons. In addition, he opposed the 1972 SALT I agreement, the Anti-Ballistic Missile Treaty, the Peaceful Nuclear Explosions Treaty of 1976, and SALT II, promising to "ship the thing back to the Soviets in Moscow."[16]

What Reagan did favor in place of arms control was achieving "overall military and technological superiority over the Soviet Union," according to the 1980 Republican Party platform. Doug Waller maintains that Reagan "advocated quick deployment of the MX (Missile Experimental) missile, production of the B-1 bomber that Carter had scrapped, renewed focus on the air defense system, accelerated development of air, ground, and sea launched cruise missiles, and increased research and development of an anti-ballistic missile system. It was nothing short of a major buildup requiring the largest military spending increase in peacetime history."[17]

Reagan repeatedly expressed the belief that the Soviet Union was an actual evil empire. In his view, the Soviets could never be trusted to negotiate in good faith and would only respond to brute force. According to Secretary of State Alexander Haig, Soviet officials were eager to negotiate with the Reagan administration but were rejected, and instead, Reagan sought to build up the nuclear arsenal.[18] The fact that Haig knew this makes it even more troubling that within the first six weeks of the Reagan administration, the secretary of state linked the Soviets to "terrorism in El Salvador and condemned them for training, funding, and equipping international terrorists," further eroding US-Soviet relations. Strobe Talbott describes Reagan as "a detached, sometimes befuddled character" who "frequently did not understand the basic aspects of the nuclear weapons issues and of the policies promulgated in his name."[19] As Henry Maar III explains, Reagan did little to put the public's mind at ease on the issue as he consistently discussed the possibility of a "limited nuclear war" in Europe.[20]

To carry out his vision, Reagan surrounded himself with hard-liners who shared his worldview and position on nuclear weapons. Vice President George H. W. Bush, Defense Secretary Caspar Weinberger, National Security Advisor Richard Allen, Central Intelligence Agency head William Casey, and United Nations Ambassador Jeane Kirkpatrick all endorsed the idea that nuclear war was winnable and that the time had come to expand the nuclear arsenal. Bush boasted of America's ability to "win" a nuclear war. Deputy Defense Secretary Frank Carlucci III told the Senate that he was seeking a "nuclear-war-fighting capability," while Louis O. Giuffrida, Reagan's head of the Federal Emergency Management Agency (FEMA), commented to ABC News that nuclear war "would be a terrible mess, but it wouldn't be unmanageable." Charles Kupperman, an appointee to the Arms Control and Disarmament Agency, declared nuclear war "a physics problem" and maintained that "it is possible for any society to survive" a nuclear war. On witnessing an underground nuclear explosion, Energy Secretary James B. Edwards told the press he found it "exciting." Conservative pundit Colin S. Gray proposed in *Foreign Policy* that when it comes to nuclear war, "Victory Is Possible." Secretary Haig pointed out that current US plans included the possibility of firing a "nuclear warning shot" somewhere in Europe if the Soviet Union were to "misbehave."[21]

Defense Secretary Caspar Weinberger took Reagan's sentiments even further when he decided to pursue a capability not just for deterring, but for "prosecuting a global war with the Soviet Union." Weinberger stressed the need to develop nuclear forces capable of winning a nuclear war—or, as National Security Council Advisor Thomas C. Reed put it, "prevailing with pride."[22] Indeed, word soon leaked of Weinberger's five-year plan calling for defense budgets that would enable the United States to win a protracted nuclear war. Weinberger then announced the production of the controversial neutron bomb on the anniversary of the atomic bombing of Hiroshima. Testifying before the US Catholic Bishops Committee in 1982, Weinberger argued that the United States could not begin substantial negotiations with the Soviet Union until it "rearmed," which would take eight years. Paul Nitze, cofounder of the Committee on the Present Danger and appointed to serve as the administration's senior negotiator on Intermediate-Range Nuclear Forces, echoed Weinberger, stating that serious arms control talks could only begin "after we have built up our forces." When asked how long that could take, Nitze responded, "Ten years."[23]

Arms negotiator Edward Rowny suggested that arms control was possible only after a prolonged period of unilateral Soviet disarmament, while Eugene Rostow, Richard Pipes (a member of the National Security Council), and others suggested that the Soviet Union would have to transform its political nature before any agreements would be possible. Pipes claimed that this was a reasonable expectation, putting the chance of nuclear war at about 40 percent. During Rostow's confirmation hearings, Senator Claiborne Pell (D-RI) asked the Arms Control and Disarmament Agency's new director whether either country might survive a nuclear war. Rostow's reply focused on the resilience of the human race, noting that "ten million casualties on one side and one hundred million on the other is not the whole of the population."[24]

Navy Secretary John Lehman proclaimed a new doctrine of deploying naval forces near Soviet territory and threatening nuclear strikes against the Soviet heartland. A Pentagon report disclosed in the *New*

York Times instructed the military services to prepare for "prevailing" in a "protracted" nuclear war.[25] Perhaps the most alarming comments came from Deputy Under Secretary of Defense T. K. Jones, who offered that "with enough shovels," Americans could survive a nuclear war; all they needed to do was "dig a hole, cover it with a couple of doors and then throw three feet of dirt on top" and citizens would be safe from radioactivity . . . if there are enough shovels to go around, everybody's going to make it."[26] Jones maintained that casualties could be limited to a mere 10 million and that the United States could recover from a nuclear war in two to four years.[27]

Once his team was in place, President Reagan began implementing the arms control policy he had promised.[28] To accomplish this, Reagan oversaw the largest nuclear buildup in American history.[29] The military budget grew from $130 billion in 1979 to nearly $300 billion in 1985, an increase of more than 50 percent above inflation. Though Reagan is often remembered as a fiscal conservative, when it came to defense, the budget was not a consideration. "You spend what you need," he argued, and in the 1980s, defense spending increased annually, from $158 billion in fiscal year 1981 to a peak of $304 billion for fiscal year 1989—a total of $2.7 trillion spent on defense. Some of these funds went toward the development of new nuclear weapons and delivery systems, including the B-1 and a new B-2 bomber, the controversial MX missile, Trident missile submarines, intermediate-range cruise missiles, and a reevaluation of nationwide nuclear civil defense plans.[30]

In addition to Reagan's own cabinet officials, conservative think tanks immediately went to work on a public relations campaign to help sell Reagan's defense spending plans. The American Security Council Foundation (ASCF), described by Henry Maar III as "a hawkish defense lobbyist organization," was founded in 1955 as a personnel security and consulting firm. Maar contends that the ASCF led the propaganda effort against détente and SALT II. The group had 320,000 members, including 231 members of Congress and President Reagan. The ASCF stored millions of files on "dissidents" and created and distributed propaganda films, brochures, and other direct mailings aimed at building support for increased defense spending and scaring the American public about the size and strength of the US military.[31]

The military buildup accomplished two things: it scared the American public into thinking we were going to have a nuclear war, and it angered Americans about where money was being spent. Reagan asked Congress for a $33.1 billion increase in defense spending for 1983. At the same time, he asked for cuts of nearly $26 billion from domestic programs. With 9.3 million Americans out of work, and another 1.2 million too discouraged to look for jobs, Reagan's budget cuts had the greatest effect on the most vulnerable: minorities and the working class.[32]

Due to Reagan's "voodoo economics," as Vice President Bush once called it, the economy got worse during the early years of Reagan's presidency. Unemployment increased from an average of less than 7 percent under Carter to 10.7 percent early in 1982, and it was substantially worse for women and minorities. Although inflation was substantially cut, ultimately reaching negative numbers in early 1983, interest rates skyrocketed, dramatically increasing the real cost of credit to more than 14 percent in early 1982.[33]

Reagan's focus on building up his nuclear arsenal had an especially dramatic effect on children. His administration significantly reduced spending on the Aid to Families with Dependent Children (AFDC) program, food stamps, child-nutrition programs, maternal and child health programs, and family planning. Federal funds for day care were sharply cut back as were training and employment programs such as the Comprehensive Employment and Training Act (CETA), which was eliminated. In the early 1980s, 24 percent of children under the age of six lived in poverty. Free school lunches were eliminated for more than one million poor children, who depended on the meal for as much as half of their daily nutrition. Over twelve million children entered the ranks of the officially declared "poor." Black children were four times as likely as white children to grow up on welfare, which was reduced to $500–$700 a month, leaving them well below the poverty level of about $900 per month. In Michigan, where the unemployment rate was the highest in the country, the infant death rate began to rise in 1981. In parts of Detroit, one-third of children were dying before their first birthday.[34]

The buildup led some Americans to believe the country was gearing up for nuclear war, and fears were on the rise. Historian George C.

Herring assessed Reagan's first term as a period when "the Cold War re-escalated to a level of tension not equaled since the Cuban Missile Crisis." Polling data confirms that by the end of 1981, 47 percent of Americans believed that nuclear war was possible. The *Bulletin of the Atomic Scientists* moved the hands of the "doomsday clock" on its cover to four minutes to midnight in 1982. A year later, close to half of all Americans still believed that they may die in a nuclear war.[35] Liberals, who normally had nothing good to say about Richard Nixon, recalled favorably the détente he maintained with the Soviet Union.[36] George Kennan, the former diplomat and prominent Soviet historian, claimed that "the public discussion of the problems presented by nuclear weaponry which is now taking place in this country is going to go down in history as the most significant that any democratic society has ever engaged in."[37]

Examining nuclear culture in the 1980s, William Knoblauch convincingly shows the impact Reagan's rhetoric and the newly awoken antinuclear movement had on the American people. "The March 29, 1982 cover of *Time* featured an alarming image: a billowing mushroom cloud with a sinister face. *Time*'s headline story, 'Thinking about the Unthinkable,' reflected the rising levels of nuclear fear in America," he writes. The author, James Kelly, noted that as of that month, "from the halls of Congress to Vermont hamlets to the posh living rooms of Beverly Hills, Americans are not only thinking about the unthinkable, they are opening a national dialog on ways to control and reduce the awesome and frightening nuclear arsenals of the superpowers."[38]

In the same month, *Publishers Weekly* featured a piece titled "A Checklist of Nuclear Books," which editor Joann Davis labeled "Fear Books." Indeed, throughout the early 1980s, an increasing number of antinuclear nonfiction books educated Americans on the dangers of nuclear weapons and helped to galvanize citizens to rally in June 1982. To put this phenomenon in context, *Newsweek* noted that between 1979 and 1983, more than 130 antinuclear books entered the literary marketplace. *The Unforgettable Fire*, which displayed art of atomic bomb survivors, and Jonathan Schell's *The Fate of the Earth*, which warned about the dangers of the arms race in vivid detail, both became required reading, according to Knoblauch. Once Reagan was elected, increased sales of the books proved to publishers that readers were interested in antinuclear literature. When Schell's book topped best-seller lists, it inspired *Nuclear War: What's In It For You?*, a book by the antinuclear group Ground Zero, which became an important promotional and organizational tool for a nationwide "Ground Zero Week."[39]

The nuclear issue also appeared in a new medium: Music Television (MTV). Beginning in 1981, one could not watch an hour of MTV without seeing or hearing messages about nuclear weapons and the end of the world from nuclear war. As Tom Nichols explains, Australian pop stars Men at Work's video for "It's a Mistake" featured Soviet and American generals playing soldiers like little boys and accidentally starting World War III. Genesis's video for "Land of Confusion" depicted Ronald Reagan as a puppet who wakes up from a nightmare and accidentally hits the button labeled "nuke." The viewer is then shown a mushroom cloud. Sting's song "Russians" is entirely about the arms race, with lyrics stating in part, "Mr. Reagan says we will protect you, but I don't subscribe to that point of view." Nuclear weapons, the Cold War, and President Reagan simply could not be ignored in popular culture.[40]

In addition to fearing nuclear war, nuclear power became a new concern in the late 1970s. Organized by the Clamshell Alliance, thousands of antinuclear demonstrators staged a nonviolent occupation of the Seabrook, New Hampshire nuclear reactor site in April 1977, leading to 1,400 arrests. This led to the emergence of similar groups around the country, including the Catfish Alliance in Alabama, the Oystershell Alliance in New Orleans, the Cactus Alliance in Utah and Arizona, and the Abalone Alliance in California. The issues of nuclear testing, nuclear power accidents, and radioactive waste began to weigh heavily on the minds of Americans. Jerome Price suggests that the accident at the Three Mile Island (TMI) nuclear reactor in Pennsylvania in March 1979 provided a much-needed boost to the antinuclear cause.[41] Henry Maar III agrees, arguing that TMI provided a "dramatic spark" to the "environmental wing" of the antinuclear movement. Pregnant women, infants, and toddlers within twenty miles were told to evacuate, while those within ten miles of the plant were ordered to stay indoors. In the wake of the TMI accident, "No more Harrisburgs!" became a rallying cry, Maar writes.[42]

Moreover, an unlined earthen dam at the United Nuclear Corporation mill tailings facility near Church Rock, New Mexico, collapsed and released 1,100 tons of radioactive tailings and 94 million gallons of toxic wastewater into the Puerco River. At the same time, the Nuclear Weapons Facilities Task Force (NWFTF) emerged as one of the most active groups in the nuclear disarmament movement. According to Paul Rubinson, NWFTF brought much-needed attention to the damage caused by nuclear power and testing. When the NWFTF formed in 1978, it had trouble appealing to disarmament activists because most NWFTF supporters saw nuclear power as a more urgent concern.[43] NWFTF members later explained the work it took to enable this shift in priorities. "This wasn't always an easy task given the antinuclear power movement's reticence to raise weapons issues, fearing they would be hindered by 'national security baggage,'" the leaders for NWFTF remembered. "We persisted, and by 1979 a new coalition was being forged with environmentalists toward challenging the more fundamental nuclear threat—nuclear weapons and nuclear war." As in previous eras, protesters continued to argue that nuclear weapons were dangerous not only because they increased the likelihood of nuclear war but because they continued to harm the people they were meant to protect. The NWFTF emphasized that US nuclear weapons were being used "on our own people" through the testing, production, and deployment processes and publicized these effects on veterans, Native Americans, and residents who worked and lived near nuclear power plants and testing facilities.[44] Public faith in nuclear technology dropped, and a visceral fear of radiation spread through society. With antinuclear sentiment already on the rise, it spiked even higher and became more generalized. The public mood was ripe for a creative approach to overcoming nuclear anxiety.[45]

As a result, antinuclear groups such as SANE, Physicians for Social Responsibility (PSR), and the Union of Concerned Scientists all saw a rise in membership, and new antinuclear organizations emerged from diverse walks of life, such as the Architects for Social Responsibility, Business Executives Move, Dancers for Disarmament, Life Insurance Industry Committee for a Nuclear Weapons Freeze, Parenting in a Nuclear Age, Performing Artists for Nuclear Disarmament, Athletes United for

Peace, Blacks Against Nukes, and Social Workers for Nuclear Disarmament.[46] As William Knoblauch notes, this was not just activism by "radical kooks" or "peaceniks," but a broad coalition of citizens.

To David Cortright, SANE's former executive director, after the 1960s such a coalition was necessary: "In the late 60s and early 70s the peace movement had an aura of anti-patriotism. Our vision was more specific, and we were willing to work with the system, rather than working to bring it down . . . Now we are in the mainstream—no longer dominated by the student hippie types but rather more by the middle class, religious groups and women."[47] Helen Caldicott, who served as president of Physicians for Social Responsibility, confirmed that in the early 1980s, the American antinuclear movement was made up of "millions of people across the country arranged in disparate and individual units—churches, psychologists, lawyers, real estate brokers, artists . . . and many more." This broad-based strategy worked. In 1982, SANE's paid membership grew by 88 percent to 16,000. A nationwide survey showed that "70 percent of all Americans wanted a negotiated freeze on nuclear weapons."[48] One study put the total number of local and national peace groups in 1985 at 8,000. At PSR, membership rose from just a few hundred in 1979 to 30,000 at the end of 1984. Donors to the Council for a Livable World jumped from a low point of 7,500 in the late 1970s to 100,000 in the mid-1980s. Never before in American history had support for nuclear disarmament been so widespread. However, none could match the numbers or popularity of the nuclear freeze campaign.[49]

The freeze campaign, started by Randall Forsberg, was breathtakingly simple and profoundly significant in its political implications. It read: "The United States and the Soviet Union should adopt a mutual freeze on the testing, production, and deployment of nuclear weapons." With this modest formulation, Forsberg and the emerging nuclear freeze organizing team sparked one of the largest peace mobilizations in history.[50] With its simple call to halt the arms race, "the freeze" rapidly grew popular and, according to William Knoblauch, "certainly was a large reason why one million people flooded the streets of New York City in June 1982."[51]

The freeze proposal captured the public imagination as no other idea in the history of the atomic age had. It did so precisely because of its uncomplicated and direct message. Here was a simple and elegant proposal that cut through the confusing technical and wonky language of the arms control community and the often conflicting claims about which side was ahead. Suddenly, the problem of the arms race and the growing danger of nuclear war seemed resolvable.[52] Forsberg had sidestepped the complexities of nuclear defense strategy and appealed to common sense. Nuclear debates had often been dominated by nearly all white males, atomic jargon, an alphabet soup, and complicated game theory strategies. Forsberg had provided an alternative, one she hoped would make the freeze a "household word," and a "clear alternative to the continuing arms race."[53] The freeze was "user friendly," David Cortright writes. "You did not need a Ph.D. in physics or a degree in international relations to understand and accept the logic of the freeze. It was eagerly embraced by a public anxious for a way out of the worsening dilemma. This popular appeal of the freeze was perhaps its most revolutionary aspect. The debate over nuclear weapons and military strategy was thus radically democratized."[54] The discussion of nuclear policy was no longer relegated to Washington, DC think tanks and the Pentagon. Mainstream America was invested in the issue. The freeze was more than a specific proposal for ending the arms race. It was an assertion and a demand by ordinary citizens for a say in the most vital of all issues, the survival of the human race. By democratizing the debate on war and peace, the freeze campaign educated and empowered millions of people to work for the prevention of nuclear war.[55]

The Nuclear Freeze Steering Committee drew up a strategic plan for the period from 1980 to 1984. It called for lining up peace organizations, securing the backing of major interest groups, waging a major public education campaign to convert "Middle America," and, finally, injecting the issue into mainstream politics. The campaign's potential was indicated in November 1980 when, prematurely, a freeze resolution was placed on the election ballot in Western Massachusetts and, thanks to the efforts of Randy Kehler, Frances Crowe, and other local peace activists, it emerged victorious in fifty-nine of the sixty-two towns voting on it.[56]

Randy Kehler was instrumental in the initial freeze campaign. A veteran peace activist and founder of the Traprock Peace Center, Kehler was born in Scarsdale, New York, and graduated from Phillips Exeter

Academy and Harvard University. The Vietnam War had a profound impact on him. He refused to cooperate with the Selective Service System and instead went to work for the War Resisters League. Kehler was convicted for draft resistance and spent twenty-two months in federal prison at La Tuna, New Mexico. Kehler's time in prison only reaffirmed his desire to work for peace, which he did at the local and national levels throughout the 1970s. In 1977, Kehler was arrested for occupying the Seabrook, New Hampshire nuclear reactor site. Discussing this event, Kehler explained that for him "nuclear war was the shadow that hung over his life" since the 1960s.[57]

In early 1980, Kehler and other organizers began to educate local citizens about the nuclear freeze campaign. They collected the six thousand signatures required to qualify the referendum for the ballot, obtained endorsements from prominent politicians, and launched a vigorous voter education and turnout drive prior to election day. When the votes were counted on November 4, the freeze had won by a wide margin: ninety-four thousand voters—59 percent of the electorate—had endorsed the freeze, while sixty-five thousand had opposed it.[58]

When I asked Kehler why the freeze had such appeal, he replied: "Reagan's rhetoric about using nuclear weapons and the freeze's straightforward language. No ordinary person could understand or get excited about one hundred fewer ICBMs [intercontinental ballistic missiles]. Here was something [freeze resolution] that went right to the heart, cut right to the chase, and went beyond these little nitpicky treaties that didn't do much to put a dent in the nuclear arms race. So, these two factors came together at the same time."[59]

Continuing the effort to make the nuclear freeze mainstream, Kehler led an organization called the Nuclear Weapons Freeze Campaign (NWFC), headquartered in St. Louis. The NWFC soon had a presence in 43 states and reached tens of thousands of people. These activists tirelessly spread freeze literature, resolutions, petitions, and referenda in dozens of cities, counties, and states. As news of the success in Western Massachusetts spread, the freeze campaign gained momentum. Contributions began to flow in. One of the first came from Massachusetts businessman Al Kay, a pioneer in the development of personal computers and a former top designer with Apple. In March 1981, more than

300 people from 33 states gathered for the founding national conference of the freeze campaign at Georgetown University in Washington, DC. A year later, 159 towns in Vermont endorsed the freeze. Overall, 2.3 million Americans signed freeze petitions.[60]

In the spring of 1982, the freeze campaign in St. Louis reported some 20,000 volunteers were working in 140 offices in 47 states. Organized freeze activity was counted in 326 congressional districts. Local freeze groups formed in hundreds of communities as the new movement rapidly swept the nation. The freeze movement sparked a new sense of citizen involvement, not just in the campaign itself, but in many other peace and antinuclear groups. The result was an unprecedented increase in peace activism and a huge jump in membership and fundraising.[61]

On March 10, 1982, Senators Mark Hatfield (R-OR) and Ted Kennedy (D-MA) introduced a US Senate resolution calling for a freeze on the testing, production, and further deployment of nuclear warheads, missiles, and other delivery systems within the United States and the Soviet Union. Hatfield, a former navy lieutenant, had been one of the first US military personnel to enter Hiroshima after the atomic bombing, which had a profound effect on his thinking about nuclear weapons. Kennedy and Hatfield also proposed a significant reduction in nuclear weapons to follow the freeze. Their resolution undoubtedly helped the freeze campaign reach its peak during the 1980s.[62]

Support for a nuclear weapons freeze steadily increased throughout the early 1980s.[63] In May 1982, an AP/NBC poll showed 83 percent of Americans supported the nuclear freeze proposal. The *Washington Post* found 79 percent support for the freeze, while CBS/*New York Times* found 77 percent support. Gallup polls showed 60 percent supported it, even among such traditionally conservative groups as self-identified evangelical Christians. In the population at large, Gallup found 71 percent support for the nuclear freeze, with marginally higher support (75 percent) in the East and Midwest, among college-educated respondents, and those between 18 and 29 years old. Among professionals, Gallup found 78 percent support for the nuclear freeze, and among trade union members, 74 percent support. In all cases, support was even higher when a provision about assured verification was added and somewhat lower when the question was cast in terms of "freezing

Soviet advantages." Regardless, the message from polling was clear: a majority of the American public had had enough of the arms race.[64]

In addition to the freeze campaign, religious organizations were crucial to the antinuclear movement's resurgence. Robert Holsworth explains that although most attention has been paid to the preparation and publication of the Catholic bishops' pastoral on nuclear arms, other church communities did not neglect the nuclear issue. Holsworth mentions that various Protestant denominations endorsed the freeze and condemned further escalation of the arms race. In hundreds of localities across the nation, congregations started study groups on the relation between faith and nuclear arms, and church members debated the stance that people of faith ought to assume about the defense posture of the United States. Holsworth contends that activists from the churches were often the backbone of the movement, organizing, fundraising, licking envelopes, and writing letters to the editor.[65] Within religious circles, a proliferation of books, articles, pamphlets, and study guides had been published, providing a Christian justification for opposing nuclear weapons and taking various kinds of action against the present direction in nuclear weapons policy.[66]

Since 1945, women have played a crucial role in the antinuclear movement. While established groups like Women's International League for Peace and Freedom (WILPF) and Women Strike for Peace (WSP) had fought for nuclear disarmament throughout the Cold War, Paul Rubinson contends that a new movement emerged in the 1970s and '80s that combined feminism with nuclear disarmament. Instead of adjusting feminist ideas to fit into the antinuclear movement, the reverse happened as feminists incorporated antinuclear beliefs into their vision of the future. Indeed, a great number of activists expressed the belief that women's equality would be achieved by taking down nuclear power and nuclear weapons.[67] Dozens of groups reflected this feminist ideology. The Feminist Anti-Nuclear Task Force (FANTF), which formed in spring 1979, made nuclear power the focus of feminism. FANTF's purpose was to create "a network of radical women activists within feminism, the antinuclear, environmentalist, consumer, labor, health, disarmament and appropriate technology movements, who oppose nuclear development and espouse a feminist politics." FANTF sought alliances with women first and antinuclear activists second: "feminist organizations that work on abortion, rape, health, labor, energy and economic issues, university and city women's centers, antinuclear alliances with or without existing feminist/women's affinity groups or caucuses, disarmament/peace groups, environment and ecology groups, feminist publications and other feminist resource networks or organizations."[68]

In 1980, Helen Caldicott, an Australian pediatrician working in Boston, founded the Women's Party for Survival (WPS), which later became Women's Action for Nuclear Disarmament (WAND), in order to organize and harness the power of women in eliminating nuclear weapons. Much more than men, Caldicott argued, women rejected nuclear weapons, and WPS literature explained why, relying on fairly traditional images of women to do so: "As women, we have traditionally been assigned the responsibility of caring for and raising children. The first priority of women, throughout history and throughout the world, is the survival of our offspring, and this survival is endangered by the present militaristic policies of those in power." Women and mothers of the world "must speak with one voice" in the political realm so that "commonsense, sensitivity, nurturance, and survival, becomes predominant in U.S. policy."[69]

Caldicott is perhaps best known for her work with Physicians for Social Responsibility. The organization had been founded in 1961 to deal with the growing concern about the health effects of atmospheric nuclear testing. Caldicott combined her professional concern for the health of children with an abiding fear of the potential consequences of nuclear disaster. As she later explained, "What was the point of keeping these children alive for another five, ten or twenty years . . . when during this time they could be vaporized in a nuclear war?"[70] During most of the 1970s, the group was dormant. However, Caldicott revived it at the end of the decade. In the summer of 1978, Caldicott was working at Harvard Medical School, researching the health effects of radiation exposure. When a colleague inquired about her work, Caldicott responded: "This is a medical problem. Let's start a medical group!" In a subsequent meeting, one of the doctors mentioned PSR. Possessed by a driving sense of responsibility to save the children of the world and blessed with enormous energy and a forceful personality, Caldicott gave PSR new life and became the catalyst for a worldwide crusade to shake people out of their complacency.[71]

Hollywood agent Pat Kingsley offered to work with Caldicott for free. As a result, Caldicott was featured in *Vogue, Life, Time, Family Circle,* and *Ladies' Home Journal.* She had numerous television appearances, including *60 Minutes* and *Good Morning America.* According to Caldicott, this was a key to the success of the antinuclear movement: "Like Jefferson said, an informed democracy will have responsible factions."[72]

In the early 1980s, Caldicott set out on a whirlwind tour of lectures and speaking engagements. She crisscrossed the country and, at one point, even went to the White House for a personal meeting with Ronald Reagan. Although she was unable to shake the president's deeply held beliefs, she inspired thousands of doctors and ordinary citizens to follow in her footsteps in a new public awakening for peace.[73]

Randy Kehler explained that

> PSR did these talks from coast to coast all over in places like Idaho City and showed what would be the effects of a nuclear explosion. What would it be like in ten, twenty, fifty miles. And it was terrifying. People had no idea that an inner city could be incinerated and then people still be injured farther out. All those things came together and then there was a whole burst of new groups like Educators for Social Responsibility, Engineers for Social Responsibility, and on and on. And the whole thing just replicated itself and the thing is it could be done by a local group in town or at a national level. The whole thing was just amazing.[74]

To complement PSR's activities, Bernard Lown and Soviet cardiologist Evgueni Chazov cofounded International Physicians for the Prevention of Nuclear War (IPPNW) in 1980. The group followed Caldicott's strategy of stressing the unmanageable medical consequences of nuclear war and operated in an international context, holding conferences and meeting with groups of physicians from other nations, including those of the Eastern bloc. Well before the freeze campaign emerged, PSR ran a full-page advertisement in the *New York Times* calling for the United States and the Soviet Union to meet to discuss substantial reductions in their nuclear arsenals. With the Council for a Livable

World, PSR organized a national conference to discuss ways to end the arms race.[75]

As women redefined nuclear disarmament as fundamentally a woman's issue, members of specific professions began identifying their vocations as antinuclear at heart. Nurses, crucial as they are to the care of human beings, embraced the cause. The Nurses Alliance for the Prevention of Nuclear War held a conference at the Boston College School of Nursing on April 17, two months before the June 12 rally, titled "Nuclear War—A Nursing Dilemma." Along with nurses, doctors also mobilized to challenge the arms race.[76]

Women across the country expressed deep concern over nuclear war. At the same time, the Reagan administration was keenly aware of the attitudes of women toward nuclear weapons. In October 1980, according to the *New York Times*/CBS News poll, 36 percent of the women polled, as opposed to 26 percent of men, said they were afraid that Reagan, if elected, would involve the country in war. By March 1982, 52 percent of women said they thought the president might do so, compared to 44 percent of men. In the same month, only 39 percent of women approved of Reagan's stewardship, against 48 percent of men. Caldicott was not surprised: "We are closer to the sources of life than men are."[77]

One woman in particular, Frances Farley, became an unlikely leader against the development of the MX missile. Farley, a state senator in Salt Lake City, decided in 1980 to open a campaign against the MX missile when she concluded that the "racetrack" basing system being contemplated would mean that almost every flat space in the mountains of western Utah and Nevada would be covered by concrete loops on which the big missiles would be shifted from silo to silo. Farley, a 54-year-old grandmother, health services administrator, and Democratic candidate for Congress in Utah, founded the MX Information Center, a group that mobilized residents against the missile-basing scheme. Intense public opposition to the MX plan in the West, where Republican support had been strong, was a key factor in the administration's decision to abandon the basing proposal, according to White House officials. "My fight against the MX made me run for Congress," said Farley. "I used to say I'm not a defense expert, but I don't say that anymore."[78]

Farley was not alone. Utah governor Scott Matheson (D) and Nevada governor Robert List (R) formed a bistate commission to examine the MX missile project. Once citizens and other local politicians in Utah and Nevada made their voices heard, Matheson came out against the potential MX missile base in Utah, calling his initial support an "embarrassment." Fearing a reelection loss in 1980, Senators Paul Laxalt (R-NV) and Jake Garn (R-UT), both "defense hawks," became the Senate's leading opponents of the MX plan, according to Henry Maar III.[79] While Laxalt and Garn were surprise critics of the MX base, opposition also came from the Congressional Black Caucus (CBC). Led by Congressman Ronald Dellums (D-CA), the CBC focused on the amount of money being spent on the MX missile versus cuts to programs that benefitted the poor. Dellums went so far as to meet with Spencer Kimball, head of the Mormon Church, in Utah. Following the meeting, the church formally came out against the MX missile.[80]

Much like what was happening throughout the United States, Lawrence Wittner explains, fear of nuclear war reignited the disarmament movement around the world in the late 1970s. This only increased when Reagan took power in 1980. The new president surrounded himself with advisors who believed nuclear war was a reasonable option to deal with adversaries. As a result, poverty rose, but so did the number of citizens invested in the nuclear issue. Old antinuclear groups resurfaced. New ones formed. Activists committed themselves to freezing the nuclear arms race. Individuals who had previously been silent found their voices. The American public became educated on the dangers of nuclear weapons. The antinuclear movement had fully awoken, and the stage was set to organize the largest demonstration in United States history.

PART II

THE LAST DANCE

CHAPTER 3

Planning the Rally

On June 7, 1982, several hundred Buddhist monks from Japan, accompanied by activists and volunteers from various nations, arrived on foot at the United Nations in New York City, completing a World Peace March that had begun in Japan almost a year before. Many who took part in the march were atomic bomb survivors or had been in some way personally affected by the atomic bombings of Hiroshima and Nagasaki. By the afternoon, the crowd, which had grown considerably, gathered in Dag Hammarskjöld Plaza to hear a series of performances and speeches. Afterward, children and adults joined hands and began the Children's Walk for Life. They carried at the head of their procession the Olympic torch, which had been specially brought from Greece for the occasion.[1] At the same time, representatives from most of the 157 member states listened as UN General Assembly President Ismat T. Kittani and UN Secretary-General Javier Pérez de Cuéllar began the five-week special session in an effort to agree on a disarmament program that would halt the arms race and the march toward nuclear war. Demonstrators continued marching, circling through Midtown Manhattan and back to UN headquarters, where they laid down photos of friends and relatives. They wanted to send a strong and clear message to those inside: that the world's future depended on the United Nations Second Special Session on Disarmament (SSDII). These actions, however, were only a preview of what was to come five days later.[2]

Buddhist monks from Japan marching as part of the World Peace March, June 7, 1982

By 1980, the antinuclear movement had awoken. Old organizations reemerged and new ones formed. A majority of the American public, and indeed the world, favored nuclear disarmament. Members of the United Nations appeared to have heard the call and announced plans to meet specifically about the nuclear arms race. The nuclear freeze campaign had gotten the country primed. Now was the time to organize a mass action against the bomb.

In the winter of 1981, David McReynolds, David Cortright, Cora Weiss, and Mike Myerson, all veteran peace activists, "were shooting the breeze" when one of them mentioned that the next summer was the Second Special Session on Disarmament at the United Nations. Myerson explained, "They agreed that this was the time for a mass action."[3] "My sense was that this thing got started around Cora's [Weiss] table at least a year before," Cortright recalled. Weiss said, "Well there's going to be this special session and we need to organize a rally."[4] David McReynolds echoed this sentiment, saying, "We had a meeting in the home of someone in New York. Mike Myerson was there and a small group of others to discuss some action for the Second Special Session on Disarmament.

I had also gone to Japan for the War Resisters League and met with people, including Buddhists, about the possibility of coming to New York for a rally. There were certainly others who were involved very early, but our work started a year before."[5] When I asked Kathy Engel, a key organizer of the rally, how the idea for June 12 originated, she put it best: "Who cares? I don't think it matters. It's an ego thing. So many people were part of this. It's not about who gets credit for what. It's about how we came together and what transpired on that beautiful day. The narrative is important, but we were part of a collective."[6]

Once the decision was made to move forward, the hard part began. To pull off something of this magnitude, there would be a lot of moving parts that needed to be choreographed, including securing permits, speakers, performances, security, funds, and the location, as well as creating the right messaging. From the onset, there were many voices in the room—some with decades of experience, others who were novices to organizing. With many voices came many opinions. Leaders clashed on whether they should concentrate solely on nuclear weapons or incorporate the larger issue of US militarism. Would the demonstration focus on President Reagan specifically? What would be the goals of the rally? Would there be a hierarchy in terms of leadership? Committees? Subcommittees? And as these issues were discussed, hidden feelings of racism, homophobia, and sexism began to surface.

While it is clear that the success of the June 12 rally was due to a collective effort, if there was one person who was considered *the* organizer, Leslie Cagan was it. Born in 1947, Cagan's parents were activists, and some of her earliest memories were of attending demonstrations. She was aware of growing up in the shadow of Hiroshima and Nagasaki. As a young student in public school in New York City, it was not uncommon to participate in shelter drills and crouch under her desk in preparation for a nuclear attack. "We were told not to look out of the windows in case of exploding glass," Cagan recalls. "We wore name tags and were told that if an atom bomb was dropped, our bodies would be burned beyond recognition and the name tag is how they would identify us. That is a horrifying way to grow up, so nuclear weapons were in my consciousness very early, and I remember going to the ban the bomb demonstrations with my parents." Cagan's mother was especially active in the campaign against nuclear testing.[7]

When Cagan graduated from college in 1968, the world was on fire. As a student, Cagan had been involved in the anti–Vietnam War movement. Her motivating factor was the belief that little wars could lead to big wars, and big wars could lead to nuclear war. She viewed the Vietnam War with fear that Southeast Asia could become the next Hiroshima. All these years later, Cagan still remembers wondering if the world would end in 1962 with the Cuban Missile Crisis. For Cagan, the threat of nuclear war was an ever-present motivating factor in her decision to be an organizer.[8]

Cagan lived in Boston for a number of years, mostly through the 1970s and early '80s. She took part in organizing actions around the first United Nations Special Session on Disarmament in 1978. It was there that Cagan connected with Mobilization for Survival (MfS). She went on to become a staffer for Boston MfS and represented Boston MfS in the national structure.[9]

Mobilization for Survival was launched to combat and combine two issues: nuclear weapons and nuclear power. MfS was modeled after the Mobilization Committee to End the War in Vietnam. A coalition of more than 280 affiliated groups, MfS included forty national organizations, mostly active in the antiwar movement and opposing the nuclear threat.[10] According to David Meyer, who has written extensively on the nuclear freeze campaign, an article by antiwar veteran Sidney Lens in the *Progressive* became the impetus for organizing MfS. In a long piece outlining the history and basic tenets of US nuclear policy, Lens proclaimed, "Americans need defense against their own leadership more than they need defense against foreign invasion." He called for a "national movement with an international orientation" and for a demonstration to commemorate the upcoming UN Special Session on Disarmament. His call led to a series of meetings among veteran antiwar activists, including representatives from the War Resisters League (WRL), American Friends Service Committee (AFSC), Clergy and Laity Concerned (CALC), and Women's International League of Peace and Freedom (WILPF). Representatives from more than one hundred local, regional, and national groups attended a larger organizational meeting in April 1977 in Philadelphia. Lens, David Dellinger, Sid Peck, David McReynolds, Peggy Duff, and Daniel Ellsberg, all experienced activists in the antiwar and civil rights movements, announced the formation of MfS.[11] MfS officially launched in the middle of the year, focusing on four goals: "Zero Nuclear Weapons," "Ban Nuclear Power," "Stop the Arms Race," and "Fund Human Needs."[12]

Like Leslie Cagan, nearly four decades later David McReynolds still remembered where he was when the nuclear age began: "I was in a summer camp in Turkey when Truman dropped the atom bomb on Hiroshima. I was really young, and the idea of a new bomb destroying buildings and whole cities was truly frightening. It gave me nightmares." McReynolds, who went on to become an organizer with the War Resisters League, MfS, and the June 12 rally, sought through MfS to emphasize the links between US foreign policy and nuclear weapons.[13]

Mike Myerson, another of the main organizers of the June 12 rally, had been "a peace activist as long as he could remember." Myerson grew up in Los Angeles, and during the Korean War, his mother gathered signatures for the Stockholm Appeal, or "Ban the Bomb" petition as it was commonly known. Myerson grew up around antinuclear activism and eventually attended the University of California, Berkeley. He participated in the anti-ROTC and anti–Vietnam War protests and was an organizer for the US Peace Council and MfS.[14]

Since 1945, the church had been an important piece in the fight against nuclear weapons, and it was no different in 1980. For years, Riverside Church in New York City had been serving as a meeting place for many peace organizations trying to prevent nuclear war. With a long and rich history of social justice, Riverside is perhaps most recognized as the place where Dr. Martin Luther King Jr. formally came out against the Vietnam War. On April 4, 1967, exactly a year to the day before his assassination, King stepped up to the pulpit at Riverside Church and delivered his "Beyond Vietnam" speech, in which he gave a stinging indictment of US foreign policy, labeling the United States "the greatest purveyor of violence in the world."[15]

In 1977, Riverside became home to the Reverend William Sloane Coffin Jr., whom David Cortright describes as "one of the most eloquent and early voices to oppose nuclear weapons." Coffin was the former chaplain of Yale University before beginning a ten-year term as senior minister at Riverside Church. A longtime activist and veteran of both the civil rights and Vietnam antiwar movements, one of Coffin's first acts upon arriving at Riverside was to establish a disarmament program.[16] "Coffin chose his old friend and colleague from the antiwar movement Cora Weiss to lead the program," Cortright explains that "Weiss, who was an early member of WSP, brought tremendous talent and energy to the Riverside program." Together, Coffin and Weiss were a "winning team" and contributed greatly to building the revived disarmament movement. Weiss directed the Riverside program and assisted ministers and lay activists around the country in creating similar programs. "Ministers would come up to Riverside," Weiss recalled, "and we would sit together in the cafeteria and go over the details of how to get started: organizing conferences, raising funds, the whole business."[17] Soon after, Coffin and Weiss found themselves on the road, traveling to other cities to attend church-sponsored disarmament events. Coffin crisscrossed the country during his tenure at Riverside. Cortright argues that the Riverside disarmament program was vitally important in sowing the seeds of peace activism within the religious community, and Weiss became an important player in the June 12 demonstration.[18]

Once some of the main organizers were in place, the structure for planning the rally began to take shape. The June 12 Rally Committee was created, which included a personnel committee, a media task force, a fundraising group, "Third World" contacts, and other June 12 task forces, including religious, international, civil disobedience, and cultural. The latter four acted independently.[19]

The personnel committee consisted of Susan Blake of Peacesmith House, Mike Clark of Riverside Church, Tom DeLuca of New York MfS, Martha Friedlander of Fellowship of Reconciliation (FOR), Connie Hogarth of WILPF, David McReynolds of WRL, and John Miller of *WIN* magazine. There were seven officially hired staff members: Ritty Burchfield (associate director, International Exchange of Development Resources); Leslie Cagan (staff, Boston MfS); Ken Caldeira (applications consultant for Scientific Times Corporation); Bruce Cronin (campus organizer, Student Association of the State University); Kathy Engel (codirector, Fund for Open Information and Accountability); Deni Frand (executive assistant in Arms Control and Electoral

Politics-from "Stewart Mott and Associates"); and Joshua Hornick (research intern, Center for Defense Information).[20]

On February 9, representatives of WRL, CALC, SANE, MfS, FOR, the Catholic Peace Fellowship, and the New York Public Interest Research Group held a meeting. Organizers suggested the original name of the "Campaign for the Second United Nations Special Session on Disarmament," be dropped. There was a concerted effort not to use the word "campaign" to describe the rally committee. A week later, the group held its first official meeting, and the "June 12 Rally Committee" name became official. Organizers voted on the date, with June 12 receiving 14 votes to 7 for June 13. Much of this decision had to do with logistics. The committee had to work with the police, transit authority, and the parks commissioner to settle on an agreeable date and obtain the necessary permits. After addressing how to get people into the city and the availability of the Great Lawn in Central Park, organizers then turned to the march route. One option was to start at the United Nations and march to Central Park for the rally. Another option was to reverse it by starting in Central Park and marching to the UN for the main events.[21]

At this point, thirty cities from around the country had already heard about the potential demonstration, requested information, and planned to start organizing. Some of the first proposals put forward included having someone speak about US intervention in El Salvador, mandating that no politicians would be allowed to speak, and ensuring the LGBTQ community would be represented, as well as an equal number of men and women speakers, with one-third coming from the "Third World."[22]

A month later, on April 19, Harry Belafonte, James Taylor, Cesar Chavez, and other notable figures gathered in New York City at the offices of District 1199 of the National Union of Hospital and Health Care Employees to formally announce the June 12 rally.[23] In a statement supporting the action, Coretta Scott King declared, "Our nation has begun the largest military build-up in human history. As never before, we are confronted with the unthinkable specter of nuclear armageddon." Quoting her husband, King said, "One of the most persistent ambiguities we face is that everybody talks about peace as a goal, but among the wielders of power, peace is practically nobody's business . . . We are calling on concerned Americans to join us in New York on June 12 for a massive rally for peace and prosperity through a nuclear arms freeze," she concluded. United Farm Workers president Cesar Chavez said, "We can do what we did against the Vietnam War. People will come out and this will force a change in government policy." Moe Foner, executive secretary of District 1199, stated, "It is the people, not the Pentagon, who must be fed." "I can assure you that the Machinists will be with you on June 12," International Association of Machinists representative Dick Greenwood said.[24]

Once information began trickling in from various cities, organizers started to suspect that attendance would dwarf the rally at the first Special Session on Disarmament in 1978. As Leslie Cagan observed at the time: "Things happened in the last four years in this country and around the world that have pushed more people to the point where they want to act on these issues. The state of the world and the administration in Washington is different . . . The escalating military budget and indeed, military adventures that the present administration has already launched have significantly increased the threats and possibility of war." The size was beginning to settle in as organizers prepared for "200,000 or more people."[25]

Some of the goals put forth were to ensure the crowd consisted of a "broad cross section of the American public" that reached beyond those who were seasoned antinuclear activists and, as much as possible, to self-finance the rally. Part of that self-financing meant putting together a sales force to market food, T-shirts, and buttons and collecting contributions.[26] To that end, David Cortright announced that SANE had hired Chad Dobson to work full-time on the June 12 rally. Dobson had worked on the "Stop the MX" campaign and had extensive fundraising experience. While some wanted Dobson to immediately be brought on board, others held firm that they had a personnel committee who interviewed all potential staff hires, and therefore Dobson started as a volunteer. However, Dobson went on to become the point person on all things financial. Moreover, organizers recommended that the rally committee select an independent finance committee to draw up a budget in consultation with staff members and to direct the fundraising. The other task forces had separate finances and fundraising efforts.

Mobilization for Survival suggested that Riverside Church take over the money early on.[27] However, many groups and supporters individually fundraised. David Cortright asked SANE donors for $10 up to $20,000. That got them the start-up money. Groups around the country were also encouraged to participate in the May 8 "Dollars for Disarmament Tag Day." Those who took part collected donations and distributed tags on street corners and in the shopping districts of their respective cities and towns. The tags, which resembled standard luggage tags, advertised the march and rally, provided details such as the location, date, and time, included a few words explaining the SSDII, and read, "I gave for Preventive Evacuation on June 12." The money collected was used for local groups in each city to rent buses and seats for those individuals who did not have the money to attend.[28]

"The main money, however, came from the big concert that we put on at Nassau Coliseum a couple days before the rally," David Cortright explained. Chad Dobson already knew Jackson Browne and James Taylor from previous disarmament rallies. Dobson and Cortright used those connections to recruit other artists, and for two nights, the coliseum was sold out and netted about $200,000. "I remember Chad and I went backstage on the second night and picked up a check, deposited it, and the next morning we had it pretty much spent before the end of the day. It was a big chunk of money, and we needed it," Cortright said.[29]

In Southern California, Alliance for Survival, the largest antinuclear group in the region, received much of its financial support from "Survival Sunday" rock music festivals held each year at the Hollywood Bowl. Organizers and supporters of the June 12 rally consistently appealed to wealthy entertainers in Los Angeles, New York, and other major cities for contributions, and many responded with extraordinary generosity.[30] James Taylor contacted fellow musicians and arranged for some of the performances on June 12. Other musicians gave their time, talent, and money, including Paul Simon, Bob Dylan, Gil Scott-Heron, Bonnie Raitt, the Wailers, Tracy Chapman, Bruce Cockburn, and Pete Seeger. In dozens of ways, large and small, these artists supported the antinuclear movement and proved effective in drumming up support for the rally.[31] With so much interest and support, the rally committee needed someone to dedicate themselves to mainly organizing the arts community. Enter Kathy Engel.

Kathy Engel, one of three cultural coordinators, was tasked with gathering artists, musicians, and celebrities for the June 12 rally. Like other organizers, Engel was politicized at a young age: "My dad was a documentary filmmaker and friends with writer Grace Paley. He made a film when I was thirteen called *Dr. Spock and His Babies*, which was his way of speaking out against the Vietnam War. So I was aware, but I hadn't become an activist."[32] Right when the nuclear disarmament movement was awaking, Engel was working at the Academy of American Poets. In 1979, Engel joined her father and Grace Paley at an occupation of the Seabrook Station nuclear power plant. Engel credits that event as the beginning of her life as an activist.[33]

Two years out of college, Engel took a job with Mobilization for Survival. She admits that she was "totally ill equipped." However, "the wonderful thing was the older activist women were mostly schoolteachers and just had a faith in younger people who didn't know what they were doing. It was fantastic. I took the job because I was passionate and learned on the job." By 1982, Engel had left and was leading an organization called the Fund of Open Information and Accountability. Everything lined up when she was called to work on the June 12 rally. Engel had the passion, experience, and desire to incorporate the arts into all they were doing.[34]

Today, when the rally is mentioned, many recall the artists and musicians who performed, raised money, and contributed in some way to the effort. However, as is the case with mixing politics and celebrity, artists and athletes—then and now—are usually told to "stay in their lane" or to "shut up and dribble." As Engel made clear, "They were seen as the dessert, not the dinner." But for Engel, groups like Dancers for Disarmament and poets like Sekou Sundiata were essential, not just because of their ability to reach different audiences through different means, but also to demonstrate cultural representation. Engel came at it from a different angle because of her background as a poet and her duties for the rally. This was not always welcome. As Engel explained, she was dealing with a lot of egos. She was "young and a hired hand." To that end, Engel and fellow writers like June Jordan and Sara Miles started discussing ways to create better language and messaging for the rally. Together they came up with an alternative slogan for the rally: "The Last Dance." For Engel, there was the obvious point that if these activists did not get this demonstration right then it could literally be the last dance for the whole world. However, when the final decision was made, organizers went with a more direct message: "Reverse the Arms Race and Fund Human Needs."[35]

Engel explained that within the arts community "groups often took off in their own disciplines. One dancer came to talk to me and the next week there were 200 dancers organized. It was the same with the video and film people, and before I knew it, there was a whole group of performing artists for nuclear disarmament. They just moved forward. There was a tremendous sense of urgency and focus."[36] When recruiting celebrities, "one led to another," Engel said. She recalled speaking with Susan Sarandon's agent, which led to Roy Scheider, and so on. "Meryl Streep was active. Jackson Browne was very responsive. Rita Marley was amazing. James Taylor worked with Tamara Weiss, Cora's daughter, to recruit big names."[37]

Performing Artists for Nuclear Disarmament (PAND), which several artists (Jules Feiffer, Robert Altman, Harry Belafonte, Eliot Feld, and Harold Prince) formed in 1982, included musicians, dancers, actors, playwrights, composers, screenwriters, choreographers, producers, directors, designers, critics, technicians, and administrators. The group wrote letters to Congress, appeared on talk shows, and engaged in civil disobedience. In April, PAND members did what they do best: dancers danced, musicians played, actors acted. Between performances, actresses Colleen Dewhurst, Jill Clayburgh, Ellen Burstyn, and Meryl Streep, director Joseph Papp, and other members of the new organization told a standing-room-only audience why they supported a nuclear weapons freeze. Surprise guest James Taylor made his statement in a love song. Several hundred performing artists, famous and not-so-famous, signed membership cards and volunteered to get involved. Robert Brustein, the artistic director of the American Repertory Theater, was among the group's seventy-five sponsors. Nearly one thousand persons filled the Symphony Space theater. Others lined up along three blocks of Broadway and could not get in. "It's wonderful you were so willing to come," Burstyn shouted through a bullhorn outside. "I promise you that the next time we have a meeting, it will be in much bigger place, now that we understand the need for it."[38]

Inside, most of the actors admitted they were not used to speech-making. "I've never got up and done anything like this before," Streep admitted. "I felt," said Clayburgh, "I couldn't affect anything very much. Growing up in New York, I remember lying in bed and hearing police cars and fire trucks. I'd always be listening for that special siren which would send my family down to the basement [during a nuclear attack]. I'd lie there thinking the basement isn't deep enough, we don't have any sand-wiches, what are we going to do?" Backstage, Dewhurst told reporters she would join a sit-in at the United Nations missions of the five nuclear pow-ers. The sit-in, called "Blockade the Bombmakers," was scheduled for June 14. "We are the strength of this country," Dewhurst said, "and [our leaders] must understand from us that we run this country. We dropped that bomb but let us be the first to say to the world, we're through, to save ourselves and to save the world."[39]

"It's completely different! It's totally refreshing!" said Daniel Mc-Cusker of Dancers for Disarmament and the Lucinda Childs Dance Company. "It's the first time that I've seen so many dancers work to-gether in a noncompetitive way."[40] Dancers educated the public about nuclear war with half-dance, half-lecture pieces that were performed in public schools.

The "Invitation to Survival" was arguably the most overt political act by dancers leading up to the rally. Dancers in New York, led by David White, created a statement on disarmament and a coupon, which they managed to insert in playbills for theaters. The statement read:

> We, dancers, choreographers, and members of the dance community join with people all over the world who are horrified by the massive escala-tion of the nuclear arms race. The build-up of worldwide nuclear arse-nals and the deployment of first-strike weapons systems have brought us to the brink of the unthinkable—thermonuclear holocaust. We believe that there can be no such thing as a "limited nuclear war." It is urgent that all nations resolve not to use any nuclear weapons for any purpose;

not to build nuclear weapons for any reason; to dismantle existing nuclear weapons and find ways to deal with their wastes safely. Monies must be redirected from the military back to the servicing of human needs. We support these resolutions, and ask you, our audiences, essential members of this community, to support them with us. On June 7th, the United Nations will begin the Second Special Session on Disarmament. Many events are being planned to focus world attention on this issue. On Saturday, June 12th, people will march from the United Nations to Central Park in the largest show of support for disarmament in American history. Please join us there. You can help build a world-wide campaign to save humanity from nuclear extinction.[41]

Dancers made up a small but powerful part of the arts community that came together for June 12. Engel and the Cultural Task Force had the idea to create "sideshows" of dance, poetry, and murals for June 12 and thus worked with dancers and choreographers to perform on the streets around the United Nations. Visual artists made banners, posters, and a mobile mural for the demonstration. Artists Against Nuclear Arms raised money to place advertisements in arts periodicals and the *New York Times*. A papier-mâché team constructed an army of doves. Poetry readings were scheduled for each block and street corner around Central Park. A nationwide Disarmament Song Contest was organized. To organizers, it seemed as though the entire arts community was getting into the act.[42]

In May, PAND organized a rally that brought about 600 children and parents to Delacorte Theater in Central Park.[43] On June 6, the Bread and Puppet Theatre, along with the International Orchestra and Choruses, staged a pageant and puppet show that included a sing-along to the last movement of Beethoven's Ninth Symphony. They recruited a cast of 450 people for the show and provided song sheets for everyone. The pageant was held in St. Patrick's Cathedral, and like other SSDII activities, the crowd overflowed the three-thousand-seat hall.[44]

Engel was not the only person working twelve-hour days on the rally. Most organizers spent hours just reaching out to ordinary citizens around the country. "We made phone calls, talked to people individually, went on the road, used mail," David McReynolds recalled. He explained:

You had to tweak your message based on who you were talking to. With churches it was a religious message. For trade unionists you had to discuss economics. But overall, we constantly pressed the need to shift the economic stress from the military to human needs. We were trying to bring a sense of sanity to a country where there were slogans like "Better Dead than Red" . . . The idea of course is insane since you cannot be free if you are all dead . . . I often talked to religious folks and explained the irony that Stalin had not been able to destroy Christianity in the Soviet Union but we could with nuclear war. We tried to humanize the Soviet Union. Not the politics and government structure, but the people, the human beings.[45]

Leslie Cagan noted that individuals from all four corners of the nation prepared to attend the rally. Speaking at the time, Cagan maintained that the strongest support would probably be in the Northeast, but "we know of people organizing in Tallahassee, New Orleans, and Baton Rouge. We got word from people in Tucson and Las Vegas, San Diego and Portland . . . There will be some caravans of people traveling from across the country to be here."[46] Cagan received letters with checks from ordinary people from around the country, who assured they would be leafletting and organizing buses. Some stated they could not make it but would be there in spirit and would "hand out stickers, folders, papers, and buttons" to promote nuclear disarmament. Others sent petitions and names of support for the rally.[47] In Ithaca, New York, the Tompkins County Nuclear Weapons Freeze Campaign in February had nearly eight hundred members who gathered 7,850 signatures in support of the rally and held regular monthly meetings with over four hundred people in attendance.[48] Various businesses even came forward to support the rally. East Coast Kefir Company in Greenfield, Massachusetts, told the rally committee that it wanted to be sure it was included as a supporter of nuclear disarmament. The business asked how it could best show support as a dairy company—a financial contribution? Listed as a supporter?[49]

A month before the rally, organizing for June 12 was happening in over five hundred cities coast to coast, and a number of international delegations were signed up to participate. Representatives from European disarmament organizations made plans to attend.[50] A Japanese delegation of 1,200 people was set to attend, bringing petitions signed by 30 million Japanese citizens calling for a world free of nuclear weapons. Weighing twenty tons and transported from Japan to the United States in three jumbo jets, these petitions were to be delivered to the secretary-general of the United Nations at ceremonies in the UN Rose Garden on June 10. At the same time, a delegation from Great Britain was set to deliver petitions signed by 1.5 million British residents. Hundreds of thousands more attendees were expected from other European countries and indeed showed up. In addition, more than 1,500 buses were chartered from Minnesota and Pennsylvania, while Massachusetts reported all available buses were sold out. Special trains were reserved from all New York City suburbs and nearby cities.[51]

Just days before, as many of the international groups were arriving in the United States, the State Department invoked the Immigration and Nationality Act and prevented nearly 500 people, including 348 Japanese citizens, from entering the country. The Immigration and Nationality Act—or the "McCarran Act" named after its chief sponsor, Senator Pat McCarran (D-NV)—was created in 1952 during the McCarthy era. "Our present laws are shot through with weaknesses and loopholes. Criminals, Communists, and subversives are even now gaining admission into this country like water through a sieve," McCarran said. As a result, individuals who were part of or supported organizations deemed "communist" or "communist fronts" were labeled unfit for entry into the United States. The Japanese contingent traveling to the US for the June 12 rally was organized by Gensuikyo, also known as the Japanese Council Against A and H Bombs, an organization closely affiliated with the World Peace Council, which the State Department argued was too closely aligned with the Soviet Union. In addition, on June 3, Kay MacPherson, former president of the Voice of Women in Canada, was making her way to New York City to address a meeting hosted by WILPF at Barnard College when she was also denied entrance into the US. MacPherson was told she was on a list of persons subject to exclusion because of affiliation with certain organizations. In response, civil libertarians filed lawsuits and protested, causing the State Department to relent and grant visas to 50 members of the World Peace Council who had been denied and allowing for the nearly 350 Japanese citizens to enter to the country.[52]

While organizers were optimistic about the amount of support they were receiving, having a coalition this large and diverse also brought with it a set of obstacles that almost destroyed the entire demonstration. David Meyer explains that from establishing an organizational structure and negotiating a political platform to agreeing on a list of speakers, internal dissension became the biggest challenge for the committee leaders.[53]

Conflicts within the June 12 coalition began to surface almost as soon as planning began, Meyer writes. In the interest of gaining a large turnout, any group interested in endorsing the demonstration was welcome to join the planning. Greenpeace, Harlem Fight Back, MfS, the Unitarian Universalist UN office, Ground Zero, the Sound-Hudson Against Atomic Development (SHAD) Alliance, Pax Christi, *WIN*, WRL, the Riverside Church, the United Church of Christ, the United States Peace Council, the Communist Workers' Party, WILPF, the United Presbyterian Church, the National Conference of Black Mayors, SANE, Maryknoll missionaries, PSR, People's Antiwar Mobilization, the Communist Party, Democratic Socialist Organizing Committee, the National Black United Front, AFSC, and the National Education Association, along with dozens of other groups, were among the endorsers.[54] As a result, a major rift developed between the older, more established peace organizations, including SANE, AFSC, FOR, and the NWFC, and a coalition of more left-leaning and minority groups.[55]

The latter group included the Reverend Herbert Daughtry's National Black United Front (BUF), the Asian American Caucus for Disarmament, Hispanics for Survival and Disarmament, and the African American Coordinating Committee. The African American Coordinating Committee served as an umbrella for groups like Harlem Fight Back, the National Alliance Against Racist and Political Repression (NAARPR), Women for Racial and Economic Equality, the National Conference of Black Lawyers, the National Tenants Organization, Black Veterans for Social Justice, the National Conference of Black Pastors, and many others. Led largely by BUF, the minority groups formed the Third World and Progressive People's Coalition (TWPPC).

The coalition also included numerous small leftist organizations whose memberships were primarily white. The group called for unilateral nuclear disarmament, an end to US military aggression in Central America, and an end to racism in the US.[56]

The TWPPC, however, did not represent all African Americans and organizations representing the global south. Although some minority organizations like the Coalition of Black Trade Unionists and the Hispanic Labor Committee expressed concern over the treatment of minority groups, they hesitated to work within the TWPPC because of its radical reputation and their desire to prevent any further splits. Simultaneously, the main rally committee had garnered some Black support, including the All-African People's Revolutionary Party.[57]

David Walker, coordinator of the African-American Executive Committee (AAEC), was convinced that "Americans of color needed to respond to the genocidal policies of the Reagan administration, especially now that it is clear how increases in the arms budget have historically proved costly to low-income Americans, particularly Blacks." Operation PUSH affairs director and June 12 codirector Jack O'Dell agreed: "June 12th represents the fulfillment of what we were saying in the Poor People's Campaign a decade ago, that the preparations for war destroys the hopes and possibilities for the poorest sections of the population."[58]

In addition to the increase of minority participation, some Black leaders wanted a stronger voice in the planning process. African American Coordinating Committee member Jitu Weusi explained, "In the past, participation of Blacks had been token in these activities." However, the Third World and Progressive People's Coalition was determined to shed light on how nuclear weapons affected minority communities.[59] The TWPPC was angered by what its leadership saw as the lack of political relevance to the more moderate approach. Joe Morrison of the South African Military Refugee Aid Fund, part of TWPPC, criticized the dominant groups: "If we water down the coalition too much, it can be diluted to the point that we haven't changed anything."[60]

The African-American Executive Committee was furious upon finding out the that some in the overall rally committee "floated the idea" of inviting New York City mayor Edward Koch to speak at the rally. David Walker made clear that that AAEC "flatly denounced the prospect of such a racist personage being officially associated with the June 12th rally." His opposition to affirmative action, support for closings of vital healthcare facilities in Black communities, and de facto support for Ronald Reagan were just a few of the examples Walker called out in reference to Koch. Moreover, the "Third World" groups were adamant in the need to point out the racist nature of the spiraling arms budget, nuclear weapons' devastating impact on the global south, and the need to transfer funds slated for military waste and destruction to human needs. They also wanted to stress that the nuclear disarmament movement should not only focus on the horror of nuclear war but also on the "increasing threat of direct and indirect U.S. military intervention into poor, struggling Third World nations," Walker stated. Walker demanded that the June 12 Rally Committee state in writing no later than June 7 that it would "absolutely not invite Koch to play any role whatsoever in the June 12 Rally."[61] The TWPPC officially stated: "Our view is that the political level of the disarmament movement must be raised and that Third World people must be involved in the leadership process. Many of us were involved in the movements of the '60s and we remember all too well the attempts of the most conservative leadership, usually backed by large sums of foundation money, to limit the political slogans to the most basic, to refuse to link one issue with another, and in the most treacherous fashion, to make the movement 'safe' for politicians to come in and lead it."[62]

Much of this did not sit well with leaders of traditional peace groups, who balked at the idea of the TWPPC having a large role in the planning process.[63] The peace groups backed away from much of this and from a broader agenda generally. Agreement about how much watering down the coalition could stand was not easy to reach. The older peace organizations had conflicts among themselves about how broadly to frame the demonstration's demands. David Meyer explains that "a difficult and long debate had produced a fragile consensus around two slogans: 'Freeze and Reverse the Arms Race' and 'Redirect Resources from the Military to Meet Human Needs.'" Even the latter slogan was problematic for some groups hesitant to risk the political controversy inherent in addressing the budget, even though the freeze campaign had earlier been eager to make this connection, Meyer writes.

"The more moderate groups were primarily interested in having the demonstration reach a wide audience that would build the movement toward the center of the political spectrum."[64] Mark Roberts of Greenpeace explained, "A significant issue was trying to attract middle America . . . this rally can't be too far left . . . I personally would like to see more right-wing and conservative groups involved."[65]

David McReynolds was also critical of the rally's inclusiveness. In January, McReynolds wrote to organizers, arguing that the peace movement's biggest mistake was inviting other groups into the decision-making process:

> If the women's movement plans a major demonstration, they pull together women's organizations. If labor wants a Solidarity march, they begin by getting the political line clear with labor groups. If Blacks march, they do not approach whites or Marxist-Leninist sects to help them plan the basic politics. Only the peace movement seems again and again to begin at the wrong point. We—the FOR, SANE, AFSC, WRL, CALC, WSP, WILPF, the Riverside program and the US Peace Council should have met, should have hammered out a political agreement, a general outline, and then asked others to come in and join us at a functional level. The SSDII is a disarmament meeting. For better or worse, it is not on energy, or civil rights, or monopoly capital, or the violation of human rights in the Soviet Bloc, or the persistent brutalization of poor Americans. It is a four-week session about disarmament. From the beginning the disarmament groups had the responsibility to take charge.[66]

McReynolds also made clear that the march was not an "anti-Reagan" rally:

> I urge those who want such a really to get down to Washington and hold it where it makes sense . . . I do blame the Soviets as well as the Americans for the arms race. I do not want a "respectable" demonstration—I want us to raise hell, to express the anger people feel at being ripped off, but that anger needs to be a universal anger against the institution of war, not just the Republican Party. (I wish liberals would keep in mind that it was their Party, the Democrats, which began the arms race escalation,

and had resumed military aid to Central America just before Reagan came into power).[67]

Addressing the "radical" faction of the demonstration, McReynolds said:

> We are not struggling just with individuals, but systems, and institutions. One of our problems is capitalism—I have no hesitation in naming it—but it wasn't capitalism that drove Vietnam into Cambodia, or China into Vietnam, or put Soviet and Chinese troops on the border of each other. I really think that those here who feel the Russians (or Chinese) never make mistakes, or must be supported at all times, are working on the wrong rally. Either that, or I'm working on the wrong rally.[68]

Things fell apart after a March 6 meeting when Greenpeace, SANE, and Riverside Church decided that they could not work with some of the left groups, most notably the Black United Front. According to David Meyer, "Art van Redmundt, of Greenpeace's Washington office, sent a letter to 37 groups proposing a new executive committee and specifically excluding the Black United Front. The demonstration had to reach a broad cross-section of people, he argued, to justify the exclusion, and 'to achieve this result the rally must appear favorable to the new mainstream constituencies.'"[69] Women's Action for Nuclear Disarmament (WAND) members notified the rally committee that they and the Women's Party for Survival were thinking of pulling out of endorsing the June 12 rally because of the inclusion of the Communist Party and the Communist Workers' Party. WAND said including these groups would "greatly affect the impact of the demonstration" and that this would only hurt the ability to "reach out to a broad base of people throughout the country with the Communist Party's inclusion."[70]

Several of the groups were uncomfortable with this approach, particularly Mobilization for Survival and the War Resisters League. These organizations had their own issues with the Black United Front, but they were sensitive to the politics of exclusion and to charges of racism against the traditional peace movement.[71] John Collins of Clergy and Laity Concerned, a group that was a founding member of the rally committee, argued that a lot of the difficulties arose out of the fact that "the peace and environmental movements tended to be white and middle class and to a certain degree racist." "Not in the sense of the KKK or that kind of thing," he said. "It's just that a lot of people in white groups don't know how to relate to and work with Third World groups."[72] Leslie Cagan explained that "if you took a random shot of the crowd it would appear overwhelmingly white. That is true. But that's hardly the whole story and part of the internal dynamics of how to connect issues." Looking back, Cagan admitted, "Some of the organizing and energy that could've gone into those communities was going more to this internal fighting."[73]

As a result, the Third World and Progressive People's Coalition split off to form its own committee. The African-American Executive Committee began planning for the June 12 rally in April. A coalition of groups, organizations, and individuals started organizing the Black community to participate and give leadership to the rally. They were clear that being involved in the organizing and leadership provided them the opportunity to educate "our people" about the intersection of "militarism and racism":

> The billions of dollars squandered on weapons of mass destruction, holding out the threat to humanity's survival, is paid for by the stark denial of economic and human rights for our people here and people of color throughout the world. In fact, the dire economic plight of masses of poor peoples, of all colors and nationalities, is directly attributable to the arms race, led, inspired and carried forth by the Government of the United States.[74]

Civil rights activist Ella Baker, James Haughton of Harlem Fight Back, the Reverend William James of the Ministerial Interfaith Association, the Reverend Timothy Mitchell of Ebenezer Baptist Church, Victor Goode of the National Conference of Black Lawyers, James Butler of American Federation of State, County, and Municipal Employees (AFSCME), and David Walker of AAEC led the planning effort.[75] "Militarism Is Racism" became their tag line. Flyers announcing a "Harlem Protest: March for Disarmament and Human Needs" explained that "more than 30% Black unemployment, cuts in federal funds to housing and hospital closing, cuts in education, daycare, and social security are going to nuclear weapons." They called for marching, not only for massive cuts in the military, but also for the Voting Rights Act, universal healthcare, and affordable housing:

> We view the arms race not only as a threat to peace, but as a racist threat to the standard of living of our people and the well-being of our communities. The infant mortality rate in central Harlem is higher than in Guinea-Bissau and 30% of our people live in housing unfit for humans. Some 50% of all people killed by police are Black people. We demand no intervention in the Third World, demand science and technology be used in the service of people, not for defense and war preparation.[76]

The AAEC sponsored "Sounds of Life, Sounds of Struggle," an event organized by Harlem Lives and held on May 30 at Marcus Garvey Park. The event, described as the "community's response to Reagan's call for death and destruction," featured the African National Congress Choir, June Jordan, Abiodun Oyewole, Rappers for Survival, Sounds of Freedom, reggae bands Breadnut and Bunny and the Dominoes, and the Rod Rodgers Dance Company.[77]

The National Organization for an American Revolution (NOAR) also endorsed the rally and planned to march. NOAR focused on organizing "people from the Black and Chicano communities." Richard Feldman of NOAR said, "We believe that the growing importance and strength of the nuclear disarmament movement involves the highly organized involvement of the local churches and the men and women from the community." They wanted James McFadden, who was born in Alabama and active in the Montgomery bus boycott, to speak. Throughout the 1950s and '60s, McFadden worked with the Student Nonviolent Coordinating Committee (SNCC) and other civil rights and Black Power organizations. In 1969, he issued the "Manifesto for a Black Revolutionary Party" with three other individuals and founded NOAR.[78]

The Detroit June 12 Rally Committee planned to send five buses to the rally. Local churches and other organizations were set to send an additional six. Detroit called for connecting the nuclear issue with social program cuts that had disproportionately hurt the Black community. They wanted a resolution passed for Black representatives to speak at the rally to address issues affecting the Black community and full support for the Third World and Progressive Peoples Coalition.[79]

Discussing the importance of minority groups' participation, Charlene Mitchell, executive secretary of the National Alliance Against Racist and Political Oppression, argued that the nuclear arms buildup "affects first and foremost, Black people and Black youth in particular." She noted that industries where African Americans had made inroads, including steel and auto, were being hit the hardest, because "less steel was being used for civilian consumption and more was going to the making of weapons. This reduced the number of jobs available outside the military industrial complex." Mitchell was convinced that the unification of "Black, white, Native American Indian, Hispanic and all other nationally-oppressed people" would result in "the biggest demonstration for peace."[80] Jack O'Dell maintained:

> There can be no survival for the human race if the arms race continues. This is the first time the peace movement has added, as a demand, the transference of resources from the military to social and job creating programs . . . Dr. King and the Poor People's Campaign were saying this during Vietnam, but the peace movement as a whole wasn't. That's why the movement didn't go past the ending of the Vietnam War. Today's connections are bringing whole new constituencies into the movement."[81]

Frank Brown of the June 12 Rally Committee agreed. Brown described "high unemployment, poor housing, educational and recreational facilities and discrimination" as "bombs that are dropped on our communities every day." "Peace issues can seem sort of mystical in the face of it all. But when we talk about cutting the military budget so that we can put money back into social programs the issue is real," he said.[82]

For many of these activists, nuclear disarmament was inextricably linked to race and colonialism. Tim McGloin, national coordinator of the Friends of the Filipino People, wrote to Leslie Cagan that while the group was planning to join the June 12 rally, McGloin was very concerned about what he deemed the lack of support for the disarmament movement in "Third World countries" and the absence of a "theme of non-intervention as a part of the purpose of the action." McGloin argued the issues were connected, considering a majority of US nuclear weapons are located in foreign bases or on off-shore submarines. "There can be no disarmament movement without addressing the issues of intervention and supporting the disarmament movements in Third World countries and Japan as well as Europe. It is shameful that the Japanese people are planning on sending 1,000 delegates to the rally and then it excludes a clear statement of support of the movements in Asia, the Pacific, and elsewhere. To exclude intervention in places like El Salvador would be a tremendous setback," he concluded.[83]

The Boston SSDII Campaign, a network working to implement the goals of the Special Session on Disarmament, made clear to the rally committee that it too was in solidarity with the "Third World countries" and groups who were "seeking to combine nuclear weapons with intervention in the Third World and racism."[84] In an April letter to Leslie Cagan, Julie Maloney of the SSDII Media Task Force expressed concern about the infighting. She endorsed the idea that US intervention in Central America and other parts of the world should be part of the June 12 rally.[85]

David Cortright maintains that he tried to convince others to be sympathetic and supportive of other causes, but for this rally he thought it was important to "focus on ending the arms race and focusing on human needs." "We talked a lot about inclusiveness, and Herb Daughtry became very involved through his network, and that was not always easy. I think there were a lot of demands for more attention to the African American community . . . to me it was a miracle that it all held together. A lot of those meetings were long, contentious, not a lot of fun, but somehow we kept plowing ahead."[86]

Complicating matters, on June 6, Israel invaded Lebanon. Joseph Gerson, a well-known and respected peace activist with the American Friends Service Committee and an antinuclear organizer in the New England area, strongly believed, along with Leslie Cagan, that the rally should address this issue. He had gone on a "fact-finding" mission in Israel and Lebanon and was disappointed that the issue was left out of the demonstration. "I called as many people as I knew who would be speaking at the rally and others close to them. The only person willing to break ranks on this danger was Norma Becker of the War Resisters League," Gerson said. Specifically regarding this omission, Gerson wrote,

"If the June 12 march was one of the greatest successes of the American peace movement, omitting what was happening in Lebanon was one of our greatest failures."[87]

Randy Kehler admitted that his thoughts on inclusiveness have evolved over the years. "I remember at one point we had a national publicity director, Patricia Williams. She was one of three or four African Americans on our 30-person national staff at the time. I remember Patricia argued that we had to take on racism and I thought we should focus sharply on the arms race." Clearly conflicted, Kehler explained that in the 1980s, he was "weary about picking up other issues, whether race or labor." He discussed various people he worked with who pushed to combine the issue of racism or labor struggles with nuclear disarmament. Many groups wanted to "hitch their wagon to the freeze movement" because of how fast it had grown and how large it had become.

> But the truth is that the freeze campaign was overwhelmingly white and middle class. And it had tons of people who had never been politically active, ever. And of my greatest satisfactions was that so many people who first got involved and became activists because of the freeze issue went on to do all sorts of things after that. Even today, I run into people all over the country who say "you know how I got my start in activism? I was part of the freeze movement." So it was great. But at the time I think we might have lost a lot of those people if we had combined disarmament with other issues.

However, forty years later, Kehler contends that "while no one can focus on every issue at once, I think it's terribly important that issues be linked together so that there can be a sense of solidarity with issue and movement groups. With the freeze campaign it didn't seem that would work out. But maybe I just hadn't evolved in my own thinking at the time."[88]

Racism was not the only issue affecting the planning of the rally. According to Leslie Cagan, part of the split was because she was a major leader of the rally and there was a "bit of homophobia." "I was an out lesbian and I think for some people, who never said it to my face but I did hear it second- and thirdhand, worried about what impact it would have if the face of the coalition was an out lesbian. So I never understood the balance of the homophobia and the anti-left if you will, the politics of it . . . but there definitely was a mix of it."[89]

The issue of homophobia was epitomized when a daylong workshop to set up outreach task forces held on February 6 did not include an LGBTQ component. Other task forces set up that day included divinity students and various community groups. Louise Bruyn, a staff member for the rally, explained that "the way we organized it was each group had to have someone to lead it. For the lesbian/gay one, we did not have somebody with us that we knew could do it." Speaking to the *Gay Community News* (*GCN*), Bruyn said she personally had done outreach when she gave a speech on peace to the Boston/Dignity group on January 24 urging them to go to the march in a bus marked "Dignity/Boston." However, the need for an LGBTQ outreach task force was brought up by feminists at a meeting of the campaign's coordinating committee, which consisted of leaders of other outreach and functional task forces. Participants at the meeting discussed the possibility of keeping a low profile on controversial issues such as LGBTQ rights, abortion, the military draft, nuclear energy, and US intervention in the global south. Some organizers feared that these topics might cause other people, particularly Catholics, to stay away from the march. But the LGBTQ community found unexpected support from Sister Sue Murphy of the high school/youth task force.

As Murphy told *GCN*,

> At some meetings we discussed goals, such as lesbian/gay rights. The Catholic position was used against this, by someone who isn't Catholic, and I got concerned because what was said wasn't exactly true. Among my order, the Sisters of Notre Dame, we wondered why lesbians and gay men weren't present in any issue of social justice. My order does not try to influence the official position, but to take public positions as a group of women, in regard to such issues as lesbian and gay rights.[90]

Despite Murphy's comments, Margaret Cerullo, who represented the newsletter task force at the meeting, told *GCN*: "The general consensus of the group was for low visibility and people said that even to have a lesbian/gay task force was to make a political statement. They didn't want anything beyond that. When they talked about doing outreach, they talked about bringing people into the campaign without taking into account who they were and without letting them have any impact." But a member of the LGBTQ community told *GCN*, "The attitude of this committee in trying to protect the public reminds me of the mother who tells the gay child who comes out to her, 'I can deal with it but don't tell your father, he'll have a heart attack.'" When presented for a vote at the March 1 general meeting, the lesbian/gay task force was officially recognized, along with three other groups: anti-draft, anti–nuclear energy, and women's services. But the general membership disagreed about the visibility of controversial issues and constituencies and the goals, structure, and outreach of the march.[91] Maida Tilchen, a reporter for the *GCN*, argued that while the antinuclear movement was growing, "the way it will be carried out makes all the difference." She asked:

> Will it be a single-issue strategy that is willing to trade things off? If they stop building nuclear weapons, will we agree to the build-up of the draft and conventional weapons? Would this help change our notions of militarism, power, and how people from different backgrounds can work together? Will it be a narrow focus event which tries to recruit among the mainstream of society, among the very people who have permitted us to get to this place?

A lot of activists care deeply about disarmament, but they also care about how we develop a movement toward it. This march may be very significant: the media and the American public may identify it as "the American peace movement," Tilchen concluded.[92]

When I asked Kathy Engel about homophobia and sexism within the organizing structure, she responded:

> Of course. But it wasn't overt. Leslie Cagan is just an extraordinary human being. People now look back on it and hold her up on a pedestal, but I think people would've treated her with a different kind of reverence and respect back then if she presented differently as a woman. I was raised to always be a powerful, independent woman, but I think because of my manner and whatever else, there were times when I was treated differently. There was a kind of sexism because I didn't assert myself as powerfully. I don't think it was across the board because there were all sorts of power dynamics happening. Class and power dynamics.[93]

Cagan explains that while sexism was present, so too were some "pretty strong women." "Cora Weiss was a force to be reckoned with," Cagan said. However, "I have some mixed feelings on it. On the one hand she's an extremely difficult personality to deal with. She wants to be in control and if she's not then it's not a good project in her eyes." Cagan also pointed out that Norma Becker, Connie Hogarth, and "other strong women who were at the forefront of organizing the rally should not be dismissed."[94]

From the outset, Engel and Cagan believed in the antinuclear movement embracing the intersectional approach. "For me, it was a no brainer that nuclear weapons and the threat of nuclear war were not a single phenomenon. They are part of the US military and our overall foreign policy," Cagan argued.[95] One problem, though, was like so many protests and rallies today, how do you do it? Engel asked, "Do you take the moment where there is a big consensus where there is something that affects us as for example like climate change and the nuclear threat? You want to unite but not have an alphabet soup." When you incorporate various causes into one rally, you run the risk of having entirely too many speakers. This happened on June 12. "Some artists did not even get on the stage," Engel recalled.[96]

How much the freeze campaign should be the focus of the rally became another issue. Even some in the press began to refer to the rally as a "freeze march," while others maintained that the freeze campaign was simply a part of the overall disarmament movement. Even today, many still refer to the June 12 rally as a freeze event. "It wasn't a freeze rally . . . That's nonsense," David McReynolds said.

> Freeze was a mass movement, and it had different elements involved in it. The original idea for the freeze was freeze the level of nuclear weapons and then begin the process of disarmament. It was never intended to leave the nuclear weapons level intact. But as the freeze movement expanded it took on a lot of political clout and drew in people from the Democratic Party and it became more mainstream. Then it became a substitute for disarmament, and people said let's freeze where we are but had no intention of going any further than that. So the original idea of the freeze was lost.[97]

Leslie Cagan also offered an opinion on the freeze campaign: "Freeze was always part of the June 12 rally, and organizationally it benefited from the march more than anything else. It was there for people to get into coming off the march when people were asking what to do next. But it's not where my heart was. I have always been an abolitionist and was in favor of the complete and total abolition of nuclear weapons and nuclear energy." In Cagan's view, while the freeze campaign was important, it did not go far enough. "We weren't polar opposites. We just had a different take on it. I honestly believe that the people involved in the freeze movement wanted to live in a world free of nuclear weapons. They just had a different tactical approach as to how to get there. But to be clear, it was a disarmament rally."[98]

As rifts of this nature began to surface, a deeper split occurred when Cora Weiss signed a letter for the June 12 Rally Committee and excommunicated the US Peace Council, WILPF, WRL, and MfS. This was stunning because WRL and MfS had really gotten a lot of the rally planning started. Weiss was concerned the press would smear the rally as being run by Communists. But McReynolds explained that that was not the case with any of these groups. Moreover, Weiss wanted sole credit for starting the rally. However, "She did not start it by herself," said McReynolds. This was coupled with the fact that Weiss was upset about the inclusion of "minority groups and more left-leaning organizations."[99]

In March, McReynolds had had enough. McReynolds had learned of Cora Weiss's attempt at what Leslie Cagan labeled "a corporate coup." According to Cagan and McReynolds, Weiss attempted to form a new "corporate" structure that would "produce the event" and exclude certain groups deemed too far to the left. This troubled organizers and caused many groups supporting the rally to threaten to pull out. In a stunning letter to staff members, McReynolds referred to Weiss as "anti-feminist" and "homophobic." He wrote that Weiss's arrogance had "burned out staff, and disrupted and delayed planning the rally."[100]

The next day, McReynolds sent a follow-up letter to the rally committee. While he admitted to "being unduly harsh on Cora," he continued to criticize her role in the demonstration. Cora could be the "chief honcho in name" but was the "central problem." "She has never organized a mass demonstration and lacks the patience to work with so many groups." While she is a "woman of charm, and with more bright ideas in an hour than I have in week," he claimed, "she is obviously not high on my list of favorite people. I have tried to work with her. Norma Becker has tried to work with her. Mike Myerson has tried to work with her. Even Don Ross finally gave up," McReynolds wrote.[101]

A couple weeks before the demonstration, there was a large meeting to air out all of the grievances and determine if the rally was going to proceed or collapse. Leslie Cagan, who was present, recalled:

> The tension was so terrible in the air and the racism was so clear, I thought to myself, am I really going to hang in there for this? But it was too close, and I thought I'm not going to quit now, but I remember feeling at that moment embarrassed to be a white person. Some really stupid things were being said, but it was a really intense moment and we hung in there and got through it.

The "corporate coup" was avoided, and planning moved forward.[102] Looking back on this period, David McReynolds explained that "the irony was that Cora's politics were close to the Communist Party in many ways. Both were pretty moderate. And Cora's politics were also close to the US Peace Council, so we never quite understood what she was trying to do. In the end, I am sure she meant the best and of course we all talk to each other now."[103]

By June 12, groups from both sides had managed to resolve their differences. Ministers from the Black United Front and some of the religious groups within the rally committee agreed "in principle" on two major Black and Third World demands: one-third minority representation in the coalition leadership and the addition of slogans condemning racism and superpower intervention in the Third World.[104] All of the groups involved were able to stick together long enough for the demonstration, but the conflicts reflected real problems within the emerging peace movement—conflicts that would not be resolved and would continue to divide the movement for years to come.[105]

Even with all of this tension, one could see the magnitude of the demonstration about three weeks before the rally. Vendors started showing up around Central Park and the United Nations. Weeks prior, people independent of the march were selling merchandise related to nuclear disarmament. The rally committee had a serious discussion on whether they should force them from the street with police help. In the end, they agreed that was not a direction they wanted to go. "They embraced it as a sign that it was going to be a big rally," according to David Cortright.[106] WILPF organized the Women of the World in Action for Peace the first week of June. The International Symposium on the Morality and Legality of Nuclear Weapons was also held the same week. The International Meeting to Formulate Proposals for UN SSDII Implementation was held on June 7. That night, a benefit was held for the rally. "Meryl Streep and the June 7th Committee" invited the public to an "Evening of Testimony for Nuclear Disarmament" at the Beacon Theatre in New York City. The evening consisted of the New York premiere of *Eight Minutes to Midnight: A Portrait of Dr. Helen Caldicott* (Caldicott was the guest of honor). Richard Dreyfuss, Dustin Hoffman, James Earl Jones, and Arthur Miller were among those who appeared.[107]

On June 8, the Welcome Rally for World Peace Marchers and an International Religious Conference occurred. The International Religious Convocation was held the day before the rally, on June 11. Around ten thousand people attended an interfaith prayer service calling for an end to the nuclear arms race at the Cathedral of St. John the Divine. More than two dozen representatives of the world's major faiths led the service, which Episcopal Bishop Paul Moore Jr. of New York called "the largest interfaith gathering ever held in this city." The worshipers spilled into the aisles and onto the steps of the Gothic cathedral, at 110th Street and Amsterdam Avenue, during the two-and-a-half-hour service. "I hope that no more bombs will be dropped on any people," said 12-year-old Noriko Tonegawa of Japan, who read a poem she had written about the atomic bomb dropped on Hiroshima. She was one of five children who told of the effects of war on their lives. At one point in the service, worshipers responded firmly, "We will remember you," as names of children killed in Hiroshima and Nagasaki were read. Most of those attending said they planned on taking part in the June 12 rally. Throughout the United Nations SSD, dozens of religious groups held vigils, prayer services, and fasts in New York.[108]

The same day, the American Friends Service Committee and WILPF organized an International Feminist Disarmament Meeting at Barnard

Feminists for a Nuclear Free Future in Central Park, June 12, 1982

College. The meeting was for "women of all nations" who "identified themselves as feminists and understand the relationship of militarism and sexism in maintaining the arms race, wanted to abolish nuclear weapons, strengthen the relationship between the East and West through feminism, and share insights about how to overcome sexism in the peace movement."[109]

"We knew from the buses and the number of leaflets we gave out that it would be big. We knew from the constant phone calls coming in. You could feel the momentum was building, but I didn't know it was going to be a million people . . . We felt it building," Engel recalls.[110] "We knew it was going to be big from the amount of buses lining up and the responses they were getting," Cagan said.

> The demand for materials, the calls coming in from all over the country and in New York City alone, and the level of interest. There was a whole nexus of activities that were planned around it the week or so leading up to June 12. The bigger things like the interfaith service and the civil disobedience on the 14th and an international conference and those are all connected one way or another to the main events of June 12. But beyond that, there were film showings and theater pieces and art displays and

dance concerts and all kinds of other stuff going on all around the city, and you begin to think this was getting out far and wide. Groups like Dancers for Disarmament were forming, and you knew something big was happening. The first really big clue though was a maybe a month before, at the negotiations with the police, one of the top police officers said he knew it was going to be big because his daughter and all her friends were coming to the demonstration. So there were signs. Did we know at first it was going to be that big? No. But that morning, the minute I arrived at the location you could tell. I was out there early by 7:00 in the morning. You could already feel the energy in the air and see people gathering. But, honestly, none of us had any idea what was coming.[111]

CHAPTER 4

June 12, 1982

As the sun began to rise, organizers who at been up all night were continuing to review last-minute details. At 7:00 a.m., Leslie Cagan and others decided to take a taxi to Central Park. As they got closer to the rally site, they could not believe what they were seeing. Hours before the official march began, "gobs of people were coming," Cagan recalled.[1] She could feel the momentum and knew it was going to be a historic day. She was right.

By early morning, thousands had already arrived. The June 12 Rally Committee had provided housing for up to four thousand people in churches, synagogues, schools, and private homes. The International Liaison Office had secured housing for an additional five thousand people. Some simply spent the night in Central Park. Over a thousand buses had been chartered to New York City. All bus charter operations in Pennsylvania and Connecticut were sold out. The twenty-seven buses carrying the Hartford contingent had left at 6:00 a.m. and parked in Queens to allow the marchers to come the rest of the way by subway. Two thousand buses in all had been chartered for the demonstration. Two full trains were on the way from Boston, and one full train was coming from Princeton. All train service on Conrail's New Jersey, New Haven, Hudson, and Harlem divisions were operating with extra cars. The Long Island Rail Road added extra cars on all lines. The Metropolitan Transit Authority (MTA) added extra cars on many of the subway lines. At the same time, 120 cyclists were on their way from Boston and New Hampshire. A small group of campers from Quebec City had spent seven days driving and hitchhiking. From just over the East River, a group bent on even more creative travel danced across the Brooklyn Bridge at dawn on Saturday. In a sense, the march was already happening. Feeder marches poured in from Brooklyn, Harlem, and other parts of New York. International delegations arrived from Japan, Europe, the Soviet Union, Zambia, Bangladesh, and many other countries.[2]

Leslie Cagan, Jack O'Dell, and Bob Muehlenkamp were in charge of the overall coordinating for the day. Thousands of volunteers were on hand to make sure everything ran smoothly. There were 1,200 peacekeepers, who had completed a three-hour training course; 300 bus greeters; 200 medical aides; 250 legal observers; 900 security personnel; 500 money collectors; 50 media personnel; 100 office volunteers; 300 sales staff; and numerous staff messengers and stagehands.[3] Miles from Manhattan, streets were closed to traffic. On Friday night, Yankee Stadium's parking lot was requisitioned to hold the two thousand buses that brought—and took home—demonstrators from hundreds of US cities.[4]

Throughout the early morning, demonstrators made their way to the United Nations carrying banners and placards; some even wore costumes. Hospital union workers, Harlem Fight Back, the New York Teachers Black Caucus, and other predominately Black groups marched down to Seventh Avenue, chanting, "We're fired up; we can't take no more." On 110th Street and Lexington, they were joined by the East Harlem contingent under the banner of Hispanics for Survival.[5] They were all heading toward the rendezvous areas around the First Avenue end of Dag Hammarskjöld Plaza, near the United Nations. The stage was on Forty-Seventh Street between First and Second Avenues.[6]

Johnstone Makatini of the African National Congress and South African representative to the United Nations kicked things off. Music from the African National Congress Choir followed. Demonstrators listened to prayers, speeches, and songs as they waited for the signal to begin marching. Randall Forsberg, the Reverend Herbert Daughtry of the Black United Front, and Ossie Davis and Ruby Dee cohosted the second segment at 10:00 a.m., when the march was to officially begin.[7]

Coretta Scott King, a long-seasoned peace activist with WILPF and Women Strike for Peace, stepped on the stage and declared:

> We have come to this great city from all across America and around the world to protest the nuclear arms race. All of our hopes for equality, for justice, economic security, for a healthy environment, depend on nuclear disarmament. Yes, we have come to protest nuclear weapons. But we have also come to New York because we have a dream. An affirmative vision shared by the great masses of people of every race, religion and nation down through the ages; it is the timeless dream of a world free from fear, not only of war or its instruments, but also of hunger or of not having a roof over one's head. Somehow, we must transform the dynamics of the world power struggle from the nuclear arms race to a creative contest to harness man's genius for making peace and prosperity a reality for all the nations of the world.[8]

The first contingent of marchers was then sent on its way, while hundreds of thousands of other demonstrators waited for their turn. Soon, gigantic columns of marchers, from over five hundred cities representing virtually every state of the nation and delegations from six continents, were filling Second, Third, Fifth, Sixth, and Seventh Avenues as they headed uptown toward Central Park.[9] Children and various groups led the march to represent the themes of the rally. Each group was given a designated starting point and carried an identifying banner with a common logo. Artists for Nuclear Disarmament created three twenty-foot banners to lead the march that read, "Abolish Nuclear Weapons, Freeze the Arms Race, Fund Human Needs." A representative of every group placed something in front of the United Nations. Speakers and different cultural events were on nearly every corner along Second Avenue.[10]

Marchers included Australians, Europeans, Filipinos, and the contingent of Japanese citizens who had walked across the United States. Nuns, Punks for Peace, ranchers, businessmen, beekeepers—old and young marched. "This is very important," said nine-year-old Gregory Barger. "If there is a nuclear war, a lot of us children will die, and some of us could be very important to the future of America."[11] One sign

Rally participants from Toronto, Canada, June 12, 1982

read, "Reagan: Give me the chance to reach your age; Nuclear Disarmament." Others read: "Freeze Reagan," "Feed the People," and "Not the War Machine." A group of women held a banner that read: "Choose life so that you and your children can live, Deut. 30:19." Russell Means from the American Indian Movement implored the crowd to "understand that if we want peace—peace on earth—we have to stop the rape and abuse of our sacred grandmother, the mother earth." Children were on parents' shoulders. People climbed light poles and trees. Veterans of the Abraham Lincoln Brigade, the group of American volunteers who fought against fascism in Spain in the 1930s, marched with a banner. Banners from Sweden, the Netherlands, the United Kingdom, and Montreal were all visible. Dr. Benjamin Spock, the famed pediatrician and antiwar activist, held hands with a family as he marched toward Central Park.[12]

On one street, the marching units in order were the Communist Party U.S.A., the Kings County Democratic Coalition, and Animators Against Armageddon, a cartoonists' group. Along the march, there were floats and balloons, jugglers, and babies in strollers. There were scientists, computer programmers, environmental activists, and religious groups of all denominations. Forty counterprotesters stood

Dr. Benjamin Spock marching to Central Park, June 12, 1982

for a time at Forty-Second Street and First Avenue with signs reading, "Build Up or Freeze to Death" and "Peace Is a Soviet Weapon of Conquest." They were no match, however, for the thousands of marchers carrying placards reading: "Choose Life," "Bread Not Bombs," "No Nukes," "Reagan Is a Bomb—Both Should Be Banned," and "A Feminist World Is a Nuclear-Free Zone." Andre Shapiro, an optics technician from Springfield, Massachusetts, said he had been protesting war since 1967. "This feels like the '60s," he said. "It feels hopeful, inspiring. I always feel like, even if nothing comes of it, it's like Custer's last stand. It's good for our souls." For the next several hours, massive rivers of marchers continued flowing into Central Park. As hundreds of thousands made their way to the Great Lawn and nearby streets, Holly Near, Jackson Browne, Joan Baez, and Linda Ronstadt performed. "They're just flopping down by any tree they can find," recalled a police officer on duty in the park.[13]

Once the first marchers reached the Great Lawn, they began to gather in front of the temporary stage. The stage was in a horseshoe shape to allow for three podiums. Speakers were directed to focus on the themes of the rally, especially the victims of nuclear weapons and policies for eliminating the arms race. The plan was to have ten major addresses, each lasting five minutes; twenty testimonials, a minute in length each; six musical performances, thirty minutes each; and various victim statements of three minutes each, all interwoven throughout the program.[14]

The official program was set to start at 1:00 p.m. with the Reverend William Sloane Coffin Jr. from Riverside Church, Winona LaDuke of the Indian Treaty Council, and actors Kathryn Walker and John Shea. Cora Weiss was a co-moderator and on stage most of the time. Winona LaDuke said, "We are here today in a massive peaceful demonstration to support the Second United Nations Special Session on Disarmament, to call for a freeze and reduction of nuclear weapons, and a transfer of military budgets to fund human needs." Three thousand silver balloons were released with the slogan "Say goodbye to nuclear weapons." As the program began, Orson Welles arrived in a limousine that pulled right behind the stage area. With a cane in his hand and a cigar in his mouth, Welles made his way to the stage. "We are, all of us, afraid and . . . his [Reagan's] trillion dollar blustering about new armaments won't cure the nightmare. It will only make it worse . . . We have two choices—life or death," Welles told the crowd. Then he added, "Do you hear that, Mr. Reagan?" A short time later, a hush of excitement swept backstage as Yoko Ono discreetly arrived on foot, wearing a black sweatshirt with the word "Imagine" in white. She declined an invitation to be introduced on stage.[15]

Helen Caldicott spoke in the early afternoon. She had three minutes to speak and, as for all her speeches, had nothing prepared. It was all ad-libbed. As she walked onto the platform and saw the oceans of faces staring back at her, she thought, "What am I going to say?" It was then that Caldicott went back to her wheelhouse. What would happen if a nuclear bomb was dropped on New York City, she asked the crowd. Caldicott began describing the medical horrors of what nuclear weapons do to people. However, the line of Caldicott's speech that truly resonated and made headlines the next day was when she declared: "There's no communist babies, no capitalist babies, a baby is just a baby."[16]

Randall Forsberg looked out over the crowd and exulted:

> We've done it. This is the biggest peacetime peace movement in the history of the United States. The politicians don't believe it yet. They will. They think this is a fad. It's not. The American people are fed up with the nuclear

arms race. We're scared of the nuclear arms race, and we should be. Until the arms race stops, until we have a world with peace and justice, we will not go home and be quiet. We will go home and organize . . . We will remember in November . . . How can we spend $20 billion a year on these stupid weapons when infant nutrition and school lunches are cut back; student loans are cut back; the elderly are forced to go without hearing aids and eat dog food; and 20 percent of the Black population is unemployed?[17]

By 2:30 p.m., the crowd had reached five hundred thousand, not counting those overflowing onto Fifth Avenue and Central Park West. "There's no way the leaders can ignore this now," said Alex Willentz, who had driven overnight from Utica, New York. "It's not just hippies and crazies anymore. It's everybody." Another woman stated, "We got rid of Lyndon Johnson, we stopped the war. This movement is much bigger. It combines the issues of bread and bombs."[18] Bruce Springsteen, Rita Marley, Chaka Khan, Toni Morrison, Harry Belafonte, Sweet Honey in the Rock, Pete Seeger, and Peter, Paul and Mary all performed or delivered remarks calling for nuclear disarmament. James Taylor and John Hall sang "Children's Cry": "How can you work? How can you play? How can you plan for a better day? When you know it all

Poster on display in the crowd at the June 12, 1982, rally

may be blown away tomorrow. Feel the earth, see the sky, hear our children's children cry. That we intend to live, and it's the bomb that had to die!" Led by an atomic bomb survivor (*hibakusha*), hundreds of thousands began chanting: "No More Hiroshimas! No More Nagasakis! No more war! Peace! Peace! Peace!"[19]

Victims of nuclear testing and the *hibakusha* were especially powerful. The Japanese were a large and moving presence in part because David McReynolds had traveled to Japan and worked to bring them to the US.[20] Over thirty million Japanese citizens signed petitions that represented their collective outrage toward the arms race and called for the banishing of nuclear weapons. Mr. Akida Ishida, 54, director general of the Hiroshima Peace Institute, pleaded, "We feel that Hiroshima is the very heart of the problem we all must learn. If everyone becomes aware of the damages and tragedies, eventually people will stand up to eliminate nuclear weapons. Americans do not know enough about the effects of radiation of the atomic bombings because the American government is not telling the people about the tragedy." Many of the police were presented with folded origami cranes, a Japanese symbol of hope.[21] Through translators, the *hibakusha* told the crowd of their firsthand account of a "living

Atomic bomb survivors marching to Central Park, June 12, 1982

inferno." James Earl Jones read from Jonathan Schell's *Fate of the Earth*. Former US Representative Bella Abzug (D-NY) spoke directly to children about growing up with the message of her father's store, "The Live and Let Live Meat Market." Richie Havens wailed on his guitar as he sang about the next world war: "Goodbye Jerusalem, Grand Canyon, Parthenon, 'cause this one's going to be the last one."[22]

Organized labor was also represented. AFSCME, the American Federation of Labor and Congress of Industrial Organizations (AFL-CIO), Machinists, Teamsters, Union of Hospital and Health Care Employees, and the Committee of Interns and Residents of NY and NJ were all present. "We've shown today that we have the ability to mobilize over one million people for disarmament in the United States of America: all we have to do now is go back home and organize," the Reverend Benjamin Chavis said. Emphasizing the need to make this a movement rather than an event, Norma Becker, an organizer for the rally and veteran peace activist, said, "We have to go back to our communities and organize to defeat the nuclear warriors in November." Members of Vermont's Bread and Puppet Theatre group portrayed "The World," "The End of the World," and "The Fight against the End of the World." "If any of you think that people don't have power, I say to you you're wrong," Elizabeth Holtzman, Brooklyn district attorney said. "It was the people of this country that forced the Government to end the war in Vietnam. It was the people of this country that forced the Government to remove a President who committed crimes in high places. The people of this country—yes, the people of this world—will make their governments listen."[23]

The Reverend William Sloane Coffin Jr. declared the beginning of "the human century" and said, "The first order of the human century is to freeze the weapons so they won't burn the people." Many speakers took a more pointedly political track, calling out President Reagan and insisting that government spending on nuclear arms be shifted to social services. Katherine Wedel, 17, left a New York hospital in her sickbed smock to join the rally. "To me, it's important to be here because the money spent on bombs could be spent on finding a cure for Addison's disease," for which Wedel was being treated.[24]

For all the infighting that occurred during the planning, the intersectional approach won. Wimmin for Womyn, an LGBTQ group for women's

Bread and Puppet Theatre Group, Central Park, June 12, 1982

liberation, and Architects for Social Responsibility were among the hundreds of different groups at the rally. Various religious denominations held banners reading, "Nuclear War Means Death to All God's Children." Quakers, Franciscans, Mennonites, and Catholic nuns and priests were all scattered throughout the Great Lawn, demanding an end to the arms race. An army of wheelchairs came up the street representing New York Disabled in Action. Members of the Congress of Senior Citizens of Greater New York were there.[25]

The official poster for June 12 further illustrated the inclusiveness of the rally. The design featured a peace dove with five legs. One leg was dressed in blue jeans with a red patch and sneakers. Another, that of an African American woman, was in a multicolored skirt. A white woman's leg was in a lavender skirt and heels. One leg had pinstriped pants, while another had puffy army-green pants and boots. When we discussed the motivation behind the piece, the artist, Seymour Chwast, explained that he was conscious of diversity and wanted to drive home the point that the rally and, to a larger extent, the nuclear issue as a whole touch all sorts of individuals—not simply white, middle-class citizens. These legs, while representing various countries, ages, sexual orientations, religions, and races, were also all part of the same dove, marching for peace.[26]

Addressing inclusiveness, Leslie Cagan explained that she always wanted the demonstration to be part of a massive movement that brought together historically divided constituencies. "It's not only

June 12, 1982, poster

about one march. It's how you use the organizing and deepen the connections and finding ways for people to participate. It's about building a movement," she said.[27] From the beginning, Cagan was thinking beyond the demonstration:

> If we do these events right, it will be important because it helps energize people to go back home and keep doing the work that needs to be done. There are any number of ways to measure success in an event like this. It will be successful in terms of the turnout, energy, spirit, politics of the day itself. If that's what happens, it would be worthwhile. I'm hoping that we can plan this activity in such a way that becomes reenergizing for people so that when they get back off the buses in their hometown, they keep doing the nitty-gritty grassroots organizing around these issues.[28]

On the day of the rally, African Americans comprised 50 percent of the leadership. When one white stage manager attempted to squeeze out "Third World members" toward the end of the day, African American leaders had him removed and replaced by a Black manager.[29] Dick Gregory said the demonstrators had come to write "the unwritten page of the constitution, dealing with the right to live free from nuclear terror."[30] The Third World and Progressive People's Coalition managed to express its concerns at the march as well. The Reverend Herbert Daughtry noted the $500 billion spent on arms annually and pointed to the impact such spending had on unemployment, hospitals, schools, transportation systems, and streets inside the United States. "This is a nation with the mightiest military machine in the world and yet it cannot feed, clothe, shelter, educate, heal, and employ its people. And the same thing is happening in other countries with insatiable military machines," he said. A member of the African National Congress charged South Africa with "developing nuclear weapons to use against Black Africans." Rubén Zamora of the Revolutionary Democratic Front of El Salvador blamed the delivery of arms instead of food to El Salvador for killing the country.[31] "America was first in dropping the bomb, first in making the neutron bomb and it's about time that we learned we must be first in dismantling the bomb," Cleveland Robinson of the Coalition of Black Trade Unionists told the crowd.[32] Moreover, the Coalition of Black Trade Unionists passed a resolution that called on the United States government to join other nations in renouncing the "first use of nuclear weapons." The group reiterated its commitment to educating citizens about the threats to human life posed by the nuclear arms race and to work toward "securing a just and lasting peace in a more prosperous world."[33]

The *New York Times* described the rally as filled with "Black and Hispanic leaders who pointed out the connection between big military budgets and reduced social programs for the poor, union leaders asking for jobs instead of costly weapons, doctors voicing concern about current radiation levels and mothers worrying about their children's future." Marchers were told of the deprivation among America's poor, oppression of the country's women, racist wars in Africa, and turmoil in El Salvador. All were related to a buildup of nuclear arms. In Harlem, ministers focused on the devastating economic effects of US military budgets and demanded nuclear disarmament. Civil rights leaders Joseph Lowry, Andrew Young, and Marian Wright Edelman all spoke. Lowery declared, "Here in the United States the official commitment to the development of new first-strike weapons systems along with a limited nuclear war strategy virtually assures a mirror image response from the Soviet Union and other nuclear powers. And so as the economy of our cities and rural areas fall victim to military spending, we drift closer to nuclear disaster." The Revered William James, president of the Ministerial Interfaith Association of Harlem, further argued: "When you take a look at the military budget and then at our decaying cities, you can see that we are already victims of war. Not only would New York be a major target of any nuclear attack, it is already a target of the military budget."[34]

Two openly gay activists also addressed the crowd. Charlotte Bunch, a nationally known feminist, author, and representative of the National Gay Task Force, told the crowd:

> I am especially proud to be here today for all the lesbians and gay men of all races, classes, and nations who have been present in movements for equality, justice, peace, and liberation for many years. We have always been here but until we began a movement for our own liberation as gay people, we were present in those movements as second-class citizens, hiding ourselves and hiding those who we loved. And you can be sure that fighting for change from behind a closet door cost us a lot; it cost us in

terms of our personal dignity and it diminished the energy that we had to give to those movements . . . Today, we are a proud and open part of this struggle. Today, we bring the energies released by our movement of love for ourselves to join in this demand to stop the nuclear arms race. We know that the forces of bigotry, fear, and violence that threaten to destroy our lives simply because of who we love are linked to the forces of militarism, prejudice, and greed that threaten to destroy this planet—denying all love, all justice, all freedom, indeed all life on earth. We understand that the demand by some for control over our intimate lives—denying each person the right to control and express her and his own sexuality and denying women the right to control over the reproduction process in our bodies—creates an atmosphere of domination and militarism as acceptable. Accepting this idea that certain groups have the right to control and violate others can only end in our day with nuclear holocaust. Something is amiss in our world . . . As we join together, there is great strength in our diversity. Too many of us have come too far—out of closets, kitchens, ghettos, and out of our isolated fears about the nuclear age—to allow this madness to destroy us now. We cannot go back. We can and must go forward to stop the arms race so we can return to the tasks of meeting human needs and expanding human capacities for life and love.[35]

David Rothenberg, member of the New York City Human Rights Commission and founder of the Fortune Society, then took to the microphone:

There are over 20 million gay men and lesbians who have been watching the clock and we have been among the marchers for social change . . . and for survival. We marched in the civil rights struggle during the 1960s, Black and white gay men and women . . . but we were invisible to you because our fears and self-hatred silenced us. In the late 1960s and early 70s, when we found our voices and self-respect, we marched with you in anti-war demonstrations—but our voices were muted when we were told that we would lessen the effectiveness of the protests by our visibility. And now we join with you, open and proud and vocal, because we have all learned, that with obliteration just around the corner, we must begin to celebrate our differences—for none of us is alike and if we can be kept divided, then we can be controlled. Gay men and lesbians, in our capacity to love, join hands with you seeking a world with new understanding and acceptance of our differences. We are here together, Black and white, Hispanics, Native Americans, Asian Americans, male and female, old and young, straight and gay, seeking an avenue away from destruction. We must survive.[36]

Late that afternoon, tens of thousands still poured in from the march. Alice McGillion, a New York City Police Department spokesperson, said there were upward of seven hundred thousand people in the park. The number kept going up as more marchers arrived.[37] "Many people never made it to the Great Lawn. By three or four in the afternoon we got reports that there were people still on the major avenues coming up. The plan had been to assemble on Second Avenue, then side streets, Forty-Seventh, Forty-Eighth, Forty-Ninth, I'm not sure how far up, then they would flow into Second Avenue and down First to Forty-Second, then to Fifth Avenue to the park. At a certain point, people were on Second, Third, definitely Madison, Fifth, Sixth, Seventh, maybe Eighth Avenue. So a lot of people never made it into the park," Cagan said.[38]

The number of people who attended the Central Park rally does not tell the whole story. Several protests were held in conjunction with the

Crowd in Central Park, June 12, 1982

June 12 demonstration. The "June Action for a Non-Nuclear and War-less World" held a mass demonstration in Tokyo. It had three slogans: 1) no US-Japan Security Treaty; 2) no nuclear weapons and power; and 3) better to have an alliance of people than a military alliance.[39] In Newcastle, Maine, a silent vigil was held, and ten area churches rang their bells in support.[40] On the West Coast, a massive "We Have a Dream" rally was held in Pasadena one week before the June 12 rally in New York. The event was sponsored by the Alliance for Survival, the Interfaith Committee for the Year of Shalom, and the Southern Christian Leadership Conference, among others. More than ninety thousand people heard from African American mayor of Pasadena Loretta Glickman; actors LeVar Burton, Mike Farrell, and Donna Mills; civil rights leader James Lawson; President Reagan's daughter Patti Davis; Muhammad Ali; and labor activist Dolores Huerta. Stevie Wonder, Bob Dylan, Stevie Nicks, Joan Baez, Joe Walsh, Linda Ronstadt, Jackson Browne, and Graham Nash performed. Addressing the thousands in attendance, Jesse Jackson declared, "We shall march until there is no more war and no more weapons. The world faces a critical choice—to freeze weapons or burn the people. We're not the only nation who ever made an atomic bomb, but we're the only nation that ever dropped one. We must wake up and tell the world, we must have peace now." Jackson urged the crowd to "choose life and choose a new president."[41] In San Francisco, a rally held at the Civic Center brought in fifty thousand people.[42]

As dusk approached, the crowd in Central Park began leaving and cleaning up after itself. Demonstrators purchased last-minute souvenir T-shirts, buttons, and bumper stickers. "History had been made, and everyone knew it," write Jennifer Warburg and Doug Lowe. "America's greatest disarmament gathering had ended. But, for the million or so demonstrators, the memories and determination to keep pushing for peace, had just begun."[43] David Cortright said, "It was like wonderment and a celebration. We were all pinching ourselves to really believe what was happening at this level. We never could've imagined. It was overwhelming."[44]

When the day had ended, police officials heaped praise on the demonstrators for their harmonious behavior, while sanitation officials applauded the demonstrators for ensuring trash was picked up and dispensed in proper containers.[45] Authorities reported that 115 people were treated at the park for minor injuries, 42 were taken to local hospitals, and 10 children were reported lost. Patrick Murphy, the police department's chief of operations, called the crowd "good natured and well-behaved." While the police did not make it easy on organizers leading up to June 12, in the end they too appeared to be moved by the day: "We're for disarmament, too, you know. We hope that today will have an effect, and that Russia will also listen. This was a piece of cake. This march was for everybody," the police stated.[46]

While media reports put the crowd size at around 700,000, the official rally committee estimated 1 million. At one point, the chief of police was backstage. Chatting with Mike Myerson, David Cortright, and Cora Weiss, he said, "There must be a million people here." Of course, it was impossible to determine the exact number. However, one thing was certain: it was the largest peace rally ever to take place on United States soil. Many marchers that day wore tags reading, "I made history." Indeed, they did, as the rally gave voice to an unprecedented social movement for peace and an end to nuclear madness. "We're extremely happy and satisfied by today's demonstration," said Leslie Cagan. "We think the unbelievable march through Midtown Manhattan and the rally represent a major turning point and a major step forward in our movement."[47] At 5:00 p.m., a steady stream was still flowing into the park. But gradually, the stream became a trickle and then reversed its direction as tired demonstrators decided to head home.[48] Summing up the day, Helen Caldicott described it simply as "joy." "A kind of joy infiltrated the whole movement. It was a beautiful march. No one left a trace of rubbish. The whole place was clean as a whistle. It was a really wonderful movement and involved everybody," she said.[49]

Two days after the rally, "a totally different type of demonstration took place and set some records of its own." The "Blockade of the Bombmakers," as it was called, involved nonviolent civil disobedience. The sit-in at the UN missions of the five major nuclear powers—the United States, the Soviet Union, Great Britain, France, and China—symbolically represented a "shut down of business as usual for the nuclear powers and the arms race," according to Warburg and Lowe.[50]

The June 14 Civil Disobedience Campaign was coordinated by the War Resisters League with sponsorship from several dozen other

Die-in, June 14, 1982

groups.[51] Campaign staff member Sharon Kleinbaum pointed out that the June 14 coalition included a wider range of issues than the mass rally. The June 12 Rally Committee limited its call to "Freeze and Reverse the Arms Race" and "Redirect Resources from the Military to Meet Human Needs." The groups sponsoring the June 14 sit-ins raised the issues of unilateral disarmament, dismantling of nuclear reactors, and non-intervention in other countries' affairs and called on nations at the SSDII to "announce a significant step to be taken immediately toward disarmament and a plan to dismantle nuclear weapons and dispose of nuclear wastes."[52]

Organizers of the demonstration "insisted that all participants be trained in nonviolent civil disobedience techniques. They also insisted that each participant belong to an affinity group that would assist one another through the entire arrest and release process. For those who met these criteria, the 'Blockade of the Bombmakers' provided an exceptional opportunity to demonstrate personal convictions about the immorality of nuclear arms—an opportunity to follow in the tradition of non-violent resistance established by Henry David Thoreau, Mohandas Gandhi, Dr. Martin Luther King, Jr., and others."[53]

Organizers worked well in advance with the police to ensure the sit-ins and subsequent arrests were without incident. "Various groups awaited their turn, entered a designated arrest area, declined to leave, and were then arrested with great mutual politeness between the arrested and arresters. Forty busses, rented by the police from the transit authority, were kept busy shuttling between the five mission headquarters and various precinct stations where each blockader was given a summons and then released. Total arrests for the day came close to 2,000—making the June 14 'Blockade of the Bombmakers' the largest action of disarmament-related, non-violent civil disobedience ever," according to Warburg and Lowe.[54] But did any of this work? Did the US and Russia hear the millions of voices calling for a world free of nuclear weapons? Would Reagan and Gorbachev change course?

PART III

ENCORE

CHAPTER 5

The Legacy of June 12 and Beyond

Days after the rally, a host of articles praising the demonstration appeared in the media. Journalists highlighted the crowd size, peaceful atmosphere, performers, and organizers. However, each writer asked the same question: Would the actions of June 12 result in any change in the nuclear arms race?

Richard Hudson, the former editor of *Disarmament Times*, covered the June 12 rally. Looking back, Hudson argued that after the rally, "everything went downhill." "The glass walls on the East River proved to be thick, and the powerful political message failed to penetrate them," Hudson wrote. He blamed inaction on the lack of political will of the United Nations and the antiquated way in which the UN makes decisions, especially in that assembly decisions are nonbinding, only recommendations, and "are often ignored by nations disapproving them." As a result, the Second Special Session on Disarmament reached no major agreements.[1]

Douglas Mattern, writing in the *Bulletin of the Atomic Scientists*, came to the same conclusion, calling June 12 a "virtual failure." Except for the launching of a World Disarmament Campaign, none of the main agenda items were adopted, he wrote. The session, organized mostly by nonaligned countries, received little support from the nuclear powers.[2] Susan Jaffe in *The Nation* suggests that the June 12 rally and Second Special Session on Disarmament (SSDII) failed. While millions marched, Jaffe argued, "the arms race didn't miss a beat. A week before the conference began, the Pentagon announced contingency plans for a five-year nuclear war." Less than a third of the delegates bothered to listen to the speeches of seventy-nine representatives of international peace groups who attended the conference as lobbyists for the preservation of civilization. The few people who were in the audience when the foreign minister of Grenada spoke heard a "stirring plea from a developing Caribbean country which is an innocent bystander to the nuclear arms race." The peace groups could have just stayed home, Jaffe concluded.[3]

The Reagan administration maintained that June 12 had no effect on nuclear policy. When asked about the rally, White House spokesman Anson Franklin said, "We don't have any comment." Franklin had no idea if Reagan, who was at Camp David the weekend of June 12, had seen any of the news reports of the rally. Defense Secretary Caspar Weinberger made clear that the demonstration would not lead to any changes in official policy. "As far as whether or not a rally of that kind will make everybody suddenly change policies or not, I think clearly the answer is no . . . These policies have to be constructed and conducted in the way that seems best to the people who are the temporary guardians or trustees of these positions," Weinberger said.[4] The comments publicly coming out of the administration, however, did not tell the whole story.

President Reagan vilified the nuclear freeze campaign and the June 12 rally from their inception. Tad Daley explains that Reagan questioned the patriotism of the demonstrators and even suggested that some of the organizers might be not just communist sympathizers, but "foreign agents."[5] However, as the antinuclear movement grew, so too did the desire for the administration to take action. "Those at the highest levels of the Reagan administration privately conceded that the antinuclear backlash was potentially the most important national security challenge facing the administration," Henry Maar III writes. As an administration official told Leslie Gelb of the *New York Times*, "Our main concern . . . is to go on the record quickly with a simple and comprehensible plan to show that the Reagan team is for peace, thus taking some of the steam out of the nuclear freeze movements in Europe and the United States." In effect, David Cortright writes, the

White House was "pushed to the bargaining table by political forces."[6] Moreover, once Congress started backing arms control initiatives, the Reagan administration began to really feel the pressure. Inside the White House, the fear was that if they did not do something on arms control, Congress will.[7]

Indeed, from administration officials to the First Lady, many close to Reagan commented that he was not only aware of the antinuclear movement but began to change course, at least in part, because of activists in the streets, concerned citizens, and congressional actions demanding an end to the arms race. David Cortright spoke with many on the public relations side of the Reagan administration. Generally speaking, they would say that "Reagan wasn't influenced by public opinion, but further on they would acknowledge that they were aware of the public concern," Cortright said.[8] According to former director of public affairs Michael Baroody, "There was a growing awareness in the White House of the nuclear issue, particularly the nuclear freeze question." After the June 12 rally, Richard Wirthlin, chief White House pollster and strategist, began to add questions about nuclear policy to his polls and included analyses about how to handle the issue in his regular meetings with the president. "The administration was paying attention to the freeze movement," according to Wirthlin. "We were measuring it. It was a consideration. It did assist in determining the basic paradigm that Americans really did seek a way to reduce tensions."[9] Wirthlin admitted that the pressure of public opinion "might have influenced the timing" of the decisions to begin negotiations. Although Wirthlin at first denied the influence of public pressure on policy formulation, he later admitted that public opinion was vital in "determining some of the timing of Reagan's policies as well as some of the tactical positioning." When asked whether this meant that policies were adjusted according to what the polls said, Wirthlin responded: "Tactically there were some adjustments." Nancy Reagan "felt strongly that changing course on nuclear policy was not only in the interest of world peace, but the correct move politically."[10] According to Tad Daley, National Security Advisor Robert McFarlane remarked, "You had to have appropriations, and to get them you needed political support, and that meant you had to have an arms control policy worthy of the name." Secretary of State George Shultz said, "Given the political climate in the U.S., we could not keep pace in modernization, production, and deployment of these deadly weapons." And President Reagan himself commented that one of his main motivations for the shift in both words and deeds was that "from a propaganda point of view, we were on the defensive."[11]

Further evidence that antinuclear activism helped push the administration to the bargaining table can be found in an internal memorandum that Eugene Rostow, the administration's first Arms Control and Disarmament Agency director, sent to National Security Advisor William Clark Jr. in early 1982. The memo urged the White House to "combine the decision about starting the Strategic Arms Reduction Treaty (START) with the problem of the freeze resolutions" in an effort to discredit the freeze campaign. Although a hard-liner and one of the founders of the Committee on the Present Danger, Rostow was increasingly concerned about what he termed "an isolationist movement" and the rising tide of antinuclear sentiment. Moving ahead with strategic arms negotiations, Rostow felt, would be a means of deflecting political criticism.[12]

As the years passed, even Caspar Weinberger seemed to change his initial position. Weinberger agreed that public pressure had an impact. While insisting that "you can't bend policy every time a few thousand people wander around in the streets," Weinberger later acknowledged that the timing of the START negotiations was influenced by domestic politics. "In a democratic society you've got to respond to what the people want in one way or another."[13]

While the Reagan administration tried everything from downplaying the antinuclear movement to attempting to co-opt it, following the June 12 rally, the once-empty rhetoric of peace became the genuine goal of an increasingly pragmatic administration.[14] A week after the June 12 rally, the president declared to the United Nations that the United States was ready to "take the next steps towards arms reduction." Discussing the president's speech, David Cortright mentions that Reagan's conclusion sounded as if he were addressing the million people who had gathered the week before in Central Park. Cortright writes: "We must serve mankind through genuine disarmament. With God's help, we can secure life and freedom for generations to come."[15]

During Reagan's second term, his administration adopted much of what the freeze campaign had advocated. He launched arms control negotiations directed not just at "freezing" but at reducing the absolute size of nuclear arsenals. He agreed with Moscow to eliminate all medium-range nuclear weapons from both Eastern and Western Europe.[16] Reagan and Gorbachev proclaimed together, "A nuclear war cannot be won and should never be fought."[17] In 1987, the world watched as the two leaders in Reykjavik, Iceland, came within an inch of eliminating all nuclear weapons and changing the world forever. However, Reagan's refusal to give up his Strategic Defense Initiative plans, or "Star Wars" as they were commonly called, ensured we would continue to live with the possibility of ending life on the planet through nuclear war. Not all was lost. Reagan and Gorbachev signed the Intermediate-Range Nuclear Forces (INF) Treaty, which eliminated US and Soviet land-based ballistic missiles, cruise missiles, and missile launchers with ranges of 500–1,000 kilometers and 1,000–5,500 kilometers. Randall Forsberg declared, "This is a victory for the peace movement." Secretary of State George Shultz disagreed: "If we had listened to the freeze movement there never would have been an INF Treaty." George H. W. Bush doubled down, and in a 1992 presidential debate, he stated, "We never would have gotten there if we'd gone for the nuclear freeze crowd."[18]

While some inside the Reagan administration conceded that the June 12 rally played a role in the president changing course, what did those who put in the time, energy, and commitment to June 12 think? When I spoke to Helen Caldicott in 2017 about the legacy of June 12, she seemed defeated:

> I left Harvard, where I could have risen in the ranks, to do this full-time because I was so worried about the threat of nuclear war. But we lost the opportunity to abolish nuclear weapons. No one talks about it, no presidential candidates mention it. We're in a mess, and that's the tragedy of my life. I failed. I wasn't quite smart enough. I was a woman, and again, older men at places like Harvard were given more credibility, and I didn't fight the powers enough and I should have. And so, I wish I'd stayed in medicine. Because now I feel we are closer to nuclear war than we've ever been before, that's for sure.[19]

Mike Myerson offered a different perspective: "It was the biggest demonstration in American history except maybe for the Women's March. I don't see one action as a be-all, end-all, even the civil rights movement. Selma was historic, but look at all that led up to it. History continues and doesn't stop. And if we had no effect on Reagan, we did have an effect on a million people. Everyone carries a memory, so yes it was a success."[20]

Kathy Engel did not think the demonstration ever got its due: "Most students don't know anything about it or what came before it." Engel then went on to discuss the immediate aftermath of the rally for organizers: "You crash afterwards. I couldn't even process it. I had nightmares. I lived right across the street from William Kunstler in a tiny apartment with my partner. I had real nightmares where I would wake up worrying about coalitions and organizing. One night I screamed out the window, 'we left the children off the stage.' We didn't know how historic it was then."[21]

"I think it helped," Randy Kehler said. "It [June 12 rally] really punched it home in people's minds, including Reagan and his administration. To have that many people on this issue taking it seriously. I think it was enormously successful. I still hear people all the time say I was there or has there been a march as big as June 12? So I give a lot of credit to those who made it happen, including Leslie Cagan."[22]

Reflecting on June 12, Leslie Cagan remarked:

I measure the success of June 12 by a number of factors. The first is by the sheer number that came out. Our goal was to make it big, and we made it as big as it could be. Our goal was to communicate that nuclear weapons were connected to other issues. One of the biggest successes was that running up to it, many groups that worked on related issues now started working on nuclear weapons. And many of those groups for years existed beyond the demonstration. So from the organizing of it to the day itself, it expanded the ongoing work of the movement, and that is the biggest and most important measure of success. I don't know how it influenced Reagan, but certainly his administration was aware. I never thought that one demonstration would change policy, but if it's part of and growing out of a movement, and it puts energy, resources, and commitment back into that movement, then yes it does have an impact . . . even though I thought it was too limited, they [the freeze campaign] did a tremendous amount of work and put into motion a lot of people. So I think all of those things combined with the demonstration being a marker in the course of that work showed that we were not some isolated fringe group. We put a million people in the streets. And how many millions more does that represent? So that does have an impact on policy whether they admit or not.[23]

Forty years later, measuring the success or failures of the antinuclear movement remains difficult. It would be easy to conclude that the antinuclear movement has failed. Since the movement's peak in the 1980s, more countries have joined the nuclear club, there remain enough nuclear weapons to end life on the planet, many arms control treaties have expired, and trillions of dollars are being spent to increase or modernize nuclear arsenals around the world. Moreover, since the end of the Cold War, the antinuclear movement has struggled to find its voice. Peace and nuclear disarmament have taken a back seat to climate change and other social justice issues. However, Michael Krepon, who cofounded the Stimson Center in 1989, argued that it is because of the disarmament community that "nuclear weapons have not been used in warfare since 1945 or tested in over two decades, with the exception of North Korea."[24] The global nuclear weapons stockpile has decreased from its peak of 70,300 in 1986 to 13,100 in 2022. The United States, which at one point had over 25,000 nuclear weapons in its arsenal, is down to approximately 5,550. Moreover, in 1991, the US and Russia signed the START I treaty, and in 2010, the New START treaty was signed and ratified; it was extended for five years in January 2021. Do these developments not collectively constitute success?

In 2003, historian Lawrence Wittner published the final volume of *The Struggle Against the Bomb*, a massive history of the international nuclear disarmament movement, concluding that the antinuclear movement had in fact prevented nuclear weapons from being used during the duration of the Cold War. "Millions of people around the world made it clear that the use of nuclear weapons was utterly unacceptable and their actions restrained world leaders at every step. In the United

States, the movement expressed the demand of citizens to have a say in the foreign policy waged in their name, as well as the public's opposition to nuclear war as an instrument of foreign policy. The movement can therefore claim credit for enabling treaties that reduced radioactive fallout, limited proliferation, and restricted certain types of nuclear weapons," Wittner writes.[25]

Perhaps the most significant indicator of success happened on January 21, 2021, when the Nobel Peace Prize–winning International Campaign to Abolish Nuclear Weapons (ICAN) accomplished what was once thought unthinkable and the Treaty on the Prohibition of Nuclear Weapons (TPNW) officially went into force. Founded in 2007 in Melbourne, Australia, ICAN engaged a broad cross-section of groups and individuals, including the voices of the *hibakusha*, to build support for a nuclear weapons ban. In 2017, over 120 nations, many from the global south, signed the "ban treaty," as it is commonly known. The treaty "bans State parties from developing, testing, producing, acquiring, possessing, stockpiling, using or threatening to use nuclear weapons."[26]

As with the freeze campaign of the 1980s, one does not need a PhD in physics to understand the TPNW. The importance of developing a message and methods to educate the larger public cannot be overstated. Throughout his life, freedom fighter and revolutionary Malcolm X would often repeat the phrase, "Make it plain." Malcolm X was one of those rare individuals who could debate in the Oxford Union (and did in 1964) and also talk about race and inequality to the "boy on the block." He knew that to make change, one cannot simply speak in academic jargon but must also reach the common man. Malcolm X had that crossover ability few possess to reach both the intellectual and the common man. The late hip-hop artist Tupac Shakur was similar in this regard. The son of a Black Panther, Shakur studied ballet, poetry, jazz, and Shakespeare at the Baltimore School of the Arts. He was also a hip-hop artist who spoke to the downtrodden and dispossessed through his music. Malcolm and Tupac understood the importance of "making it plain" in the fight for freedom and equality. "For us new ones with no experience, only with a lot of enthusiasm and engagement for this cause, ICAN was really a place where we were allowed to be a part, contribute with what we could and learn, and develop a lot," Thea Katrin Mjelstad of Norway explains. "It didn't matter if you had done this work for six months or 60 years, everyone was welcome." Tim Wright, ICAN's first volunteer, explains, "We're an intergenerational campaign. Indeed, that's one of our greatest strengths. We have octogenarians working alongside school students. No one is too young or too old to contribute to a world free of nuclear weapons." Both Wright and Mjelstad joined ICAN in their early 20s. Wright became an antinuclear activist a decade earlier. "I remember learning about the atomic bombings of Hiroshima and Nagasaki and being horrified. How could such acts be committed?" he asked.[27]

Much like the antinuclear movement in the 1980s, ICAN set out to stigmatize nuclear weapons using "humor, horror, and hope." As Ray Acheson, author of *Banning the Bomb, Smashing the Patriarchy*, explains, "While the horror of nuclear weapons is important to convey the urgency of the situation, hope is essential to drive people to action . . . Building community and networks across borders is something that antinuclear activism has always offered. ICAN routinely reinforces the idea of a transnational movement—and to include activists from countries that traditionally had not been very active in their antinuclear work." This was the same in 1982 with the Black United Front and the Third World and Progressive People's Coalition.[28]

The TPNW proves that June 12 was indeed part of a movement and not a moment. Whereas no major agreement came out of the SSDII at the United Nations in 1982, the ban treaty was the culmination of decades of organizing, marching, and educating. It was because of those such as Leslie Cagan and Randall Forsberg, and especially because of the voices of the *hibakusha*, that a new generation of international activists came together to do what a million people rallying in Central Park decades ago probably never thought was possible. The fact that nuclear weapons are now illegal is the biggest testament to the work of the antinuclear movement and its success. Does that mean the work is finished? "No," Ray Acheson said. "The TPNW is not the end. We have always envisioned it as a tool to achieve nuclear disarmament."

Although the ban treaty has provided a tool and pathway to eliminating nuclear weapons, the questions remain: Where do we go from here? What lessons can be learned from June 12?

Leslie Cagan asserted:

Now you can organize on the internet. We did this all before email. I think we had one or two computers in the office, and they were only used for finances and record keeping. While activists today have social media, we should not throw away the basic organizing tools. The next thing I would tell young activists is that it does make a difference. Not every demonstration. But from time to time, gathering masses of people together can and does make a difference. And I do think we made a difference. While policy didn't change overnight, they heard us in Washington. They knew that massive amounts of people had turned out with a disarmament message. Maybe more importantly, the groups that came together for the march stayed together and kept organizing. And I think that's one of the big positive values or reasons to have demonstrations—to help people, especially from smaller cities and rural areas to be in the space and movement together . . . to literally walk on the street together and stand shoulder to shoulder at a rally and see that you are part of something that's bigger than yourself and to take that energy into the next day, the week, year. And I think that was proven.[29]

Looking forward, Cagan explained:

It's a challenge to our imagination and creativity to find a way to articulate connections where it's not just a laundry list. It's easier to focus on just one issue, but life isn't easy. Our message needs to be clear. Our work as organizers needs to always work on more than one level. And we need to think of concrete ways that citizens can get involved so they feel they are doing something. So part of that includes writing letters to the editor, visiting members of Congress, or engaging in civil disobedience. We also need to make sure people understand how nuclear disarmament is connected to other issues and other people's emotions around those issues. We need basic political education—things like how do you read the newspaper and make sense of it. On any given day there are a lot of issues in there. I still think you need to read books. I think you need to listen, not just to a twenty-second soundbite, but longer talks about how the world works.[30]

"You know the nuclear issue is just so hard to mobilize public concern about it now. I don't know how to build the support," David Cortright declared. "Climate change, healthcare, immigration are all issues of the day. I keep asking, where is the peace movement? We need to be part of all of these other movements and bring in disarmament issues."[31]

David McReynolds echoed these sentiments, especially when discussing intersectionality. "Yes, today it [nuclear disarmament] should be combined with other issues. But the danger is then you open the door to the alphabet city of causes and you end up with nothing. One of the great insights on the march in 1963 was it was not just about civil rights. It was about jobs and freedom too. It was very important to see how those were connected. But it wasn't jobs and freedom for gays, ecology, etcetera. So I think the great genius of 1963 was combining the economic issue which was essential to Black liberation . . . so we also need to focus on the economics. Because the arms race is so tied to the economy. But I would not favor an alphabet city of a list of thirteen things that are most on your mind. I think you have to limit it to several key issues."[32]

The success of the antinuclear movement in the 1980s was also due in large part to organizing through fear and hope. Leading up to June 12, it seemed as though Helen Caldicott was everywhere. And in many ways, she was. One could not turn on the television without hearing Caldicott discussing what nuclear weapons did to human beings. Along with books showing horrific images drawn by the *hibakusha* and films like *The Day After*, fear worked. It moved people to action. Today, however, there are those who contend that the movement should not organize through fear. Moreover, some younger activists argue that today is different, especially for people of color. These organizers maintain that for many, nuclear weapons simply do not take precedence over fighting systemic racism, concentrated poverty, unequal education, climate change, unemployment, and a lack of healthcare. However, it is a mistake to assume that these issues were not present in the 1980s. The 1980s were riddled with issues that directly affected marginalized communities, from the AIDS epidemic to the War on Drugs. Police brutality was rampant in the 1980s. Yet millions, including thousands of people of color and members of the LGBTQ community, committed themselves to a world free of nuclear weapons. Why? Because for many, it did not matter if they achieved social justice if they were dead from nuclear war. They realized how these issues were connected and the message was clear.

Throughout my time writing this book, Russian leader Vladimir Putin escalated the invasion of Ukraine by putting his nuclear forces on high alert. New York City issued a public service announcement on how to "survive a nuclear attack," and the US government continued spending exuberant amounts of money on nuclear weapons. People all over the world are once again discussing nuclear war. Panic and anxiety seem to be setting in, as many are beginning to educate themselves about the nuclear threat. Seeing this all play out as I was writing about the height of the antinuclear movement made me think deeply on the nuclear issue and June 12. I thought about the words by writer Rebecca Solnit: "The true impact of activism may not be felt for a generation. That alone is reason to fight rather than to surrender into despair."[33]

The importance of June 12 is that it shows that even though problems existed throughout the organizing—some of the same problems that exist currently—and at the time it looked like nuclear war may be inevitable, millions of people in New York and, indeed, around the world refused to believe that was their fate. They organized, marched, rallied, researched, wrote, spoke, sang, and danced to ensure we would all be alive. That said, what June 12 also makes clear is that providing hope is essential. Those who attended the June 12 rally left with a feeling that they could stop this madness. They returned home motivated to organize and believed they could make a difference. And they did. They changed policy. That is significant. It matters. Or as Kathy Engel explained to me:

> There are moments and they only happen when you know that there is a righteousness and readiness and you are going to break the mold, struggle, and disagree. But humans can come together across all geographic, class, ethnic, religious, and all differences to say we are human and we want to survive . . . and we are going to do this through puppeteering, lecturing, pastoring, policy making, and by trusting the power of the people. Students need to learn that they have the power and that even if we didn't stop nuclear weapons, we did do something significant and that is really important. We are not just living in the moment. We don't measure our ability to have an impact in the short time we are on this planet. It's not a linear measurement. It's the power of the human spirit

and the belief that there are enough of us to stand in the street together just like the Arab Spring. We are at a moment where we have to galvanize people. As amazing as June 12 was, now we should do something different. Not sure what, but we should take from the best of what we did and evolve. We can be much more imaginative. Where we are now, I believe we are forced to act. We are primed.[34]

ACKNOWLEDGMENTS

As I learned from my first book, setting off on a journey to research a subject and write about it for years is not something one can do alone. Throw in a global pandemic, and there was no way this book would have been completed without the support, patience, and love from those around me. I have been fortunate that throughout my career I have had scholars, writers, and experts in the field who have been there to push, advise, and champion me along the way. These individuals supported my work, offered suggestions to make it stronger, and pushed me to think deeply about the subject matter. To David Ekbladh, Jim Strick, Zia Mian, Ray Acheson, Lovely Umayam, Sean Meyer, Togzhan Kassenova, Nick Roth, Sylvia Mishra, Ambassador Bonnie Jenkins, Michelle Dover, Becky Alexis-Martin, and Daryl Kimball, I am deeply thankful for your expertise, friendship, and support. This book is better because of all of you.

Working on this book during the pandemic made me appreciate my friends and family even more than I already did. I would like to sincerely thank Shelby Parish, Eric Singer, John Pitonzo, Dave Zirin, Terrence Robinson, Desmond and Sheena Meade, Dave and Erin Stoker, John and Gretchen McCourt, Liam Delaney, Jackie DeLeon, Donna and Tony Intondi, and Tracy and Alexis Greene for all your love and support. I would especially like to thank my wife, Natalie. There is no one who knows me better. Whether it was telling me to walk away from the laptop always at the right moment, taking over "dog duty" while I wrote and edited, listening to me drone on about the antinuclear movement in the 1980s, or reminding me why this book had to be written, I am eternally grateful, and there will never be enough words to describe how honored and thankful I am that she chose me.

As a graduate student, I devoured everything Martin J. Sherwin wrote. I got to know Marty after he served on my dissertation committee in 2009. He was one of my strongest advocates when I wrote my first book, *African Americans Against the Bomb*, and I could not have been prouder when it became part of his series on nuclear studies at Stanford University Press. Through the years, I continued to learn from Marty about nuclear issues and how to be a better writer. Before he died, Marty made clear that he wanted this book to be in his series with Johns Hopkins

University Press. I know how lucky I am and do not take for granted that I had the opportunity to work with Marty on not one, but two books. I was devastated when he passed and wish he could have read the final product. Marty was a treasure and a giant in the nuclear studies field. I will always be thankful to him for the opportunities he gave me, and I hope I made him proud.

Chapter 1 · Introduction

1. Lanset, "WNYC Covers the Great Anti-Nuclear March and Rally."
2. Montgomery, "Throngs Fill Manhattan," 1; Cortright, *Peace Works*, 5.
3. Feron, "Momentum Gains on Nuclear-Limit Rally," WC1; Herman, "Protesters Old and New Forge Alliance for Antinuclear Rally," B6.
4. Feron, "Momentum Gains on Nuclear-Limit Rally," WC1; Herman, "Protesters Old and New Forge Alliance for Antinuclear Rally," B6.
5. Engel, "Donald Trump: I Would Bomb the Sh-t Out of ISIS"; LoBianco, "Donald Trump on Terrorists."
6. Gerzhoy and Miller, "Donald Trump Thinks More Countries Should Have Nuclear Weapons"; Gaouette and Starr, "Facing Growing North Korea Nuke Threat"; Mount, "Biden Nuclear Posture Review," 7.
7. Maar, *Freeze!*, 4–6.
8. Intondi, *African Americans Against the Bomb*; Rubinson, *Rethinking the American Antinuclear Movement*, 116–124.
9. Maar, *Freeze!*, 16.
10. Rubinson, *Rethinking the American Antinuclear Movement*, 116.
11. Rubinson, *Rethinking the American Antinuclear Movement*, xii.
12. D. D. Guttenplan, "Who Is Jack O'Dell?" *The Nation*, August 11, 2014, https://www.thenation.com/article/archive/who-jack-odell/.

Chapter 2 · The Movement Awakens

1. Waller, *Congress and the Nuclear Freeze*, 21–22.
2. Cortright, *Peace Works*, 11–12.
3. Waller, *Congress and the Nuclear Freeze*, 21–22; Cortright, *Peace Works*, 11–12; Knoblauch, *Nuclear Freeze in a Cold War* 6; Meyer, *Winter of Discontent*, 151.
4. Wittner, *Toward Nuclear Abolition*, 1–3, 7–8.
5. Intondi, *African Americans Against the Bomb*, 87–88; Wittner, "Forgotten Years," 435; Wittner, *Toward Nuclear Abolition*:1–3, 7–8.

6. Intondi, *African Americans Against the Bomb*, 85–86.

7. Wittner, "Forgotten Years," 449.

8. Wittner, "Forgotten Years," 440.

9. Wittner, "Forgotten Years," 441.

10. Intondi, *African Americans Against the Bomb*, 90–91; Wittner, "Forgotten Years," 450.

11. Knoblauch, *Nuclear Freeze in a Cold War*, 1–2.

12. Knoblauch, *Nuclear Freeze in a Cold War*, 2.

13. Meyer, *Winter of Discontent*, 69.

14. Waller, *Congress and the Nuclear Freeze*, 13–14; Meyer, *Winter of Discontent*, 72; Cortright, *Peace Works*, 7–8.

15. Cortright, *Peace Works*, 7–8.

16. Waller, *Congress and the Nuclear Freeze*, 14.

17. Waller, *Congress and the Nuclear Freeze*, 14.

18. Cortright, *Peace Works*, 8.

19. Maar, *Freeze!*, 48.

20. Maar, *Freeze!*, 48.

21. Badash, *Nuclear Winter's Tale*, 4–5; Waller, *Congress and the Nuclear Freeze*, 16–19; Cortright, *Peace Works*, 9; Knoblauch, *Nuclear Freeze in a Cold War* 3; Meyer, *Winter of Discontent*, 72; Gray and Paine, "Victory Is Possible," 14–27.

22. Waller, *Congress and the Nuclear Freeze*, 16–19; Cortright, *Peace Works*, 9; Knoblauch, *Nuclear Freeze in a Cold War* 3; Meyer, *Winter of Discontent*, 72.

23. Cortright, *Peace Works*, 9.

24. Meyer, *Winter of Discontent*, 72.

25. Cortright, *Peace Works*, 9.

26. Knoblauch, *Nuclear Freeze in a Cold War* 3.

27. Meyer, *Winter of Discontent*, 72–73.

28. Meyer, *Winter of Discontent*, 69.

29. Knoblauch, *Nuclear Freeze in a Cold War*, ix.

30. Knoblauch, *Nuclear Freeze in a Cold War*, 5; Cortright, *Peace Works*, 9.

31. Maar, *Freeze!*, 46–47.

32. "Support for UN Special Session on Disarmament," Californians for a Bilateral Nuclear Freeze, n.d. Leslie Cagan Papers, UNSSDII: Affiliated Activities, US, NYU.

33. Meyer, *Winter of Discontent*, 58.

34. Sidel, *Keeping Women and Children Last*, xii–xiv; Zinn, "Reagan's Economic Policies Favored the Rich," 69–70; See also Nunez, *A Shelter Is Not a Home or Is It?*; Marable, *How Capitalism Underdeveloped Black America*; Phillips, *Politics of Rich and Poor*.

35. Knoblauch, *Nuclear Freeze in a Cold War*, 5.

36. Badash, *Nuclear Winter's Tale*, 4–5.

37. Holsworth, *Let Your Life Speak*, 6.

38. Knoblauch, *Nuclear Freeze in a Cold War*, 1.

39. Knoblauch, *Nuclear Freeze in a Cold War*, 12, 23.

40. Nichols, "I Want My Mutually Assured Destruction."

41. Jerome Price, "The American Antinuclear Movement Evolves: 1970–1990," in Smith, *Antinuclear Movement*, 106–107.

42. Maar, *Freeze!*, 31.

43. Rubinson, *Rethinking the American Antinuclear Movement*, 116; Schwab, *Radioactive Ghosts*, 58.

44. Rubinson, *Rethinking the American Antinuclear Movement*, 116.

45. Cortright, *Peace Works*, 10.

46. Rubinson, *Rethinking the American Antinuclear Movement*, 116.

47. Knoblauch, *Nuclear Freeze in a Cold War*, 6.

48. Knoblauch, *Nuclear Freeze in a Cold War*, 6.

49. David Richardson, "On the March," 24–26; Cortright, *Peace Works*, 15–17; Knoblauch, *Nuclear Freeze in a Cold War*, 6.

50. Cortright, *Peace Works*, 12.

51. Knoblauch, *Nuclear Freeze in a Cold War*, ix.

52. Cortright, *Peace Works*, 12

53. Knoblauch, *Nuclear Freeze in a Cold War*, 7.

54. Cortright, *Peace Works*, 12.

55. Cortright, *Peace Works*, 12.

56. Cortright, *Peace Works*, 14.

57. Wittner, *Toward Nuclear Abolition*, 29; Cortright, *Peace Works*, 13–14.

58. Cortright, *Peace Works*, 14.

59. Randy Kehler, interview by author, June 2, 2017.

60. Rubinson, *Rethinking the American Antinuclear Movement*, 117.

61. Cortright, *Peace Works*, 16–17.

62. Smith, *Antinuclear Movement*, 62.

63. Cortright, *Peace Works*, 86.

64. Meyer, *Winter of Discontent*, 88; Butterfield, "Anatomy of the Nuclear Protest," SM14.

65. Holsworth, *Let Your Life Speak*, 17.

66. Holsworth, *Let Your Life Speak*, 17.

67. Rubinson, *Rethinking the American Antinuclear Movement*, 121.

68. Rubinson, *Rethinking the American Antinuclear Movement*, 121.

69. Rubinson, *Rethinking the American Antinuclear Movement*, 122.

70. Helen Caldicott, interview by author, April 7, 2017; Wittner, *Toward Nuclear Abolition*, 73.

71. Helen Caldicott, interview by author, April 7, 2017; Wittner, *Toward Nuclear Abolition*, 73.

72. Helen Caldicott, interview by author, April 7, 2017.

73. Cortright, *Peace Works*, 27.

74. Randy Kehler, interview by author, June 2, 2017.

75. Meyer, *Winter of Discontent*, 102.

76. Rubinson, *Rethinking the American Antinuclear Movement*, 127.

77. Miller, "3 Women and the Campaign for a Nuclear Freeze."

78. Miller, "3 Women and the Campaign for a Nuclear Freeze."

79. Maar, *Freeze!*, 31.

80. Intondi, *African Americans Against the Bomb*, 111.

Chapter 3 · Planning the Rally

1. Warburg and Lowe, *You Can't Hug With Nuclear Arms*; Minutes of Rally Committee Meeting, April 19, 1982, UNSSDII: June 12, NYC: Rally Committee Meetings, Leslie Cagan Papers, TAM #138, Box 10. The Olympic torch was brought from Greece, through Europe to Canada. Runners carried the torch from Montreal to the US border. About five thousand runners from the US, with help from various athletes, including players from the National Football League (NFL) brought the torch to New York City.

2. Warburg and Lowe, *You Can't Hug With Nuclear Arms*.

3. Mike Myerson, interview by author, July 7, 2017.

4. David Cortright, interview by author, March 3, 2017.

5. David McReynolds, interview by author, July 3, 2017.

6. Kathy Engel, interview by author, July 6, 2017.

7. Leslie Cagan, interview by author, June 1, 2017.

8. Leslie Cagan, interview by author, June 1, 2017.

9. Leslie Cagan, interview by author, June 1, 2017.

10. Meyer, *Winter of Discontent*, 147.

11. Meyer, *Winter of Discontent*, 147.

12. Wittner, *Toward Nuclear Abolition*, 30; Wittner, "Forgotten Years," 444.

13. David McReynolds, interview by author, July 3, 2017.

14. Mike Myerson, interview by author, July 7, 2017.

15. Martin Luther King Jr., "Beyond Vietnam," April 4, 1967, Martin Luther King, Jr., Research and Education Institute, Stanford University, www.kinginstitute.stanford.edu.

16. Cortright, *Peace Works*, 42.

17. Cortright, *Peace Works*, 42–43.

18. Cortright, *Peace Works*, 42–43.

19. Proposal on Campaign Structure; UNSSD Meeting Minutes, February 9, 1982, UNSSDII: June 12, NYC: Rally Committee Meetings, Leslie Cagan Papers, TAM #138, Box 10.

20. UNSSD Meeting Minutes, February 9, 1982, UNSSDII: June 12, NYC: Rally Committee Meetings, Leslie Cagan Papers, TAM #138, Box 10.

21. UNSSD Meeting Minutes, April 19, 1982, UNSSDII: June 12, NYC: Rally Committee Meetings, Leslie Cagan Papers, TAM #138, Box 10.

22. UNSSD Meeting Minutes, April 19, 1982, UNSSDII: June 12, NYC: Rally Committee Meetings, Leslie Cagan Papers, TAM #138, Box 10.

23. Leslie Cagan to Rally Committee Members, April 12, 1982, UNSSDII: June 12, NYC: Rally Committee Meetings, Leslie Cagan Papers, TAM #138, Box 10.

24. Trinkl, "Plans Build for Disarmament Rally," 3, UNSSDII: June 12, NYC: Press Coverage, Leslie Cagan Papers, TAM #138, Box 10.

25. Murray Rosenblith, "An SSD Preview," *WIN*, May 15, 1982, 16–17, UNSSDII: Affiliated Activities, United States, Leslie Cagan Papers, TAM #138, Box 10.

26. UNSSD Meeting Minutes, March 1, 1982, UNSSDII: June 12, NYC: Rally Committee Meetings, Leslie Cagan Papers, TAM #138, Box 10.

27. UNSSD Meeting Minutes and Personnel Report, February 17, 1982, UNSSDII: June 12, NYC: Rally Committee Meetings, Leslie Cagan Papers, TAM #138, Box 10.

28. "Dollars for Disarmament Tag Day Proposal," January 25, 1982, UNSSDII: Affiliated Activities, United States, Leslie Cagan Papers, TAM #138, Box 10; David Cortright, interview by author, March 3, 2017.

29. David Cortright, interview by author, March 13, 2017.

30. Cortright, *Peace Works*, 66.

31. Cortright, *Peace Works*, 68.

32. Kathy Engel, interview by author, July 6, 2017.

33. Kathy Engel, interview by author, July 6, 2017.

34. Kathy Engel, interview by author, July 6, 2017.

35. Kathy Engel, interview by author, July 6, 2017.

36. Rosenblith, "An SSD Preview," 16–17.

37. Kathy Engel, interview by author, July 6, 2017.

38. Susan Jaffe, "Performing Artists Rally for a Nuclear Arms Freeze," *Boston Globe*, April 7, 1982, 6, UNSSDII: June 12, NYC: Press Coverage, Leslie Cagan Papers, TAM #138, Box 10.

39. Jaffe, "Performing Artists Rally for a Nuclear Arms Freeze," 6.

40. Rosenblith, "An SSD Preview," 16–17.

41. Joshua Homick, "Dancing for Disarmament," *June 12th News*, April 6, 1982, 3, UNSSDII: June 12, NYC: Flyers, Literature, Leslie Cagan Papers, TAM #138, Box 10.

42. Homick, "Dancing for Disarmament," 3.

43. Florence Falk, "Performing Artists for Nuclear Disarmament," *Performing Arts Journal* 6, no. 2 (1982): 110; "Performing-Arts Group for Atom Curb Formed," *New York Times*, April 4, 1982, 55.

44. Rosenblith, "An SSD Preview," 16–17.

45. David McReynolds, interview by author, July 3. 2017.

46. Rosenblith, "An SSD Preview," 16–17.

47. UNSSDII: June 12 NYC: Correspondence, Leslie Cagan Papers, TAM #138, Box 10.

48. Tompkins County Nuclear Weapons Freeze Campaign to June 12 Rally Committee, February 24, 1982, UNSSDII: June 12 NYC: Correspondence, Leslie Cagan Papers, TAM #138, Box 10.

49. S. Brian Wilson to June 12 Rally Committee, May 12, 1982, UNSSDII: June 12 NYC: Correspondence, Leslie Cagan Papers, TAM #138, Box 10.

50. Trinkl, "Plans Build for Disarmament Rally," 3.

51. New York June 12 Disarmament Campaign Press Release, May 25, 1982, UNSSDII: June 12 NYC: Media Task Force, Press Releases, Leslie Cagan Papers, TAM #138, Box 10.

52. David Margolick, "Reprise on McCarran Act," *New York Times*, June 4, 1982, B1, B6; Peter Kihss, "U.S. Is Said to Bar 500 Who Seek Visas to U.N. Disarmament Parley," *New York Times*, June 3, 1982, A1, A10; Kihss, "50 in Peace Group to Get Visas," B1, B6.

53. Meyer, *Winter of Discontent,*.185.

54. Meyer, *Winter of Discontent*, 185.

55. Meyer, *Winter Discontent*, 185.

56. "National Sponsors of the June 12th Rally," April 19, 1982, SANE Papers, Series G, Box 67, SCPC; David Lindorff, "War in Peace: The Fight for Position in New York's June 12 Disarmament Rally," *Village Voice*, April 20, 1982, 12; Pamela Mincey, "Afro-Americans Get Set For June 12," *Daily World*, February 25, 1982, p. 3.

57. "National Sponsors of the June 12th Rally"; Lindorff, "War in Peace," 12; Mincey, "Afro-Americans Get Set For June 12," 3.

58. June 12 Rally Committee Press Release, "Third World Groups March and Rally on June 12th," n.d., UNSSDII: June 12 NYC: Media Task Force, Press Releases, Leslie Cagan Papers, TAM #138, Box 10.

59. Lindorff, "War in Peace," 12; Mincey, "Afro-Americans Get Set For June 12," 3.

60. Meyer, *Winter of Discontent*, 186.

61. David Walker to June 12 Rally Committee, June 1, 1982, UNSSDII: June 12, NYC: Rally Committee Meetings, Leslie Cagan Papers, TAM #138, Box 10.

62. Lindorff, "War in Peace," 13.

63. At one point, the split became so wide that Gordon J. Davis, the city's parks commissioner, was given two separate applications for a rally permit. Mincey, "Afro-Americans Get Set For June 12," 3, 7; Herman, "Protesters Old and New Forge Alliance," B6; "Summation of the June 12 Executive Committee Meeting," March 30, 1982, SANE Papers, Series G, Box 67, SCPC.

64. Meyer, *Winter of Discontent*, 186.

65. Meyer, *Winter of Discontent*, 186.

66. David McReynolds, Memo on the Events in June, January 30, 1982, SANE Papers, Series G, Box 67, SCPC.

67. McReynolds, Memo on the Events in June, January 30, 1982, SANE Papers, Series G, Box 67, SCPC.

68. McReynolds, Memo on the Events in June, January 30, 1982, SANE Papers, Series G, Box 67, SCPC.

69. Meyer, *Winter of Discontent*, 186.

70. Diane D. Aronson to June 12 Rally Committee, February 17, 1982, UNSS-DII: June 12 NYC: Correspondence, Leslie Cagan Papers, TAM #138, Box 10.

71. Meyer, *Winter Discontent*, 186.

72. Lindorff, "War in Peace," 13–14.

73. Leslie Cagan, interview by author, June 15, 2017.

74. African-American Executive Committee (SSD II) letter to supporters, April 1982, UNSSDII: June 12, NYC: African-American Executive Committee, Leslie Cagan Papers, TAM #138, Box 10.

75. African-American Executive Committee (SSD II) letter to supporters, April 1982.

76. African-American Executive Committee (SSD II) flyers, UNSSDII: Affiliated Activities, United States, Leslie Cagan Papers, TAM #138, Box 10.

77. Sounds of Life, Sounds of Struggle flyer, UNSSDII: Affiliated Activities, United States, Leslie Cagan Papers, TAM #138, Box 10.

78. Richard Feldman to Bruce Cronin, March 17, 1982, UNSSDII: June 12 NYC: Correspondence, Leslie Cagan Papers, TAM #138, Box 10.

79. Glen Janken to June 12 Rally Committee, May 13, 1982, UNSSDII: June 12 NYC: Correspondence, Leslie Cagan Papers, TAM #138, Box 10.

80. Mincey, "Afro-Americans Get Set For June 12," 7.

81. De Nitto, "June 12 Buildup Gaining Support," 2.

82. De Nitto, "June 12 Buildup Gaining Support," 10.

83. Tim McGoin to Leslie Cagan, May 13, 1982, UNSSDII: June 12 NYC: Correspondence, Leslie Cagan Papers, TAM #138, Box 10.

84. UNSSDII: Affiliated Activities, United States, Leslie Cagan Papers, TAM #138, Box 10.

85. Julie E. Maloney to Leslie Cagan, April 5, 1982, UNSSDII: June 12 NYC: Correspondence, Leslie Cagan Papers, TAM #138, Box 10.

86. David Cortright, interview by author, March 3, 2017.

87. Joseph Gerson, interview by author, April 13, 2017; Meyer, *Winter of Discontent*, 188.

88. Randy Kehler, interview by author, June 2, 2017.

89. Leslie Cagan, interview by author, June 1, 2017.

90. Maidia Tilchen, "Lesbians, Gays and the UN Disarmament March," *Gay Community News*, March 20, 1982, 3. UNSSDII: June 12, NYC: Press Coverage, Leslie Cagan Papers, TAM #138, Box 10.

91. Tilchen, "Lesbians, Gays and the UN Disarmament March," 3.

92. Tilchen, "Lesbians, Gays and the UN Disarmament March," 3.

93. Kathy Engel, interview by author, July 6, 2017.

94. Leslie Cagan, interview by author, June 17, 2017.

95. Leslie Cagan, interview by June 15, 2017.

96. Kathy Engel, interview by author, July 6, 2017.

97. David McReynolds, interview by author, July 3, 2017.

98. Leslie Cagan, interview by June 15, 2017.

99. David McReynolds, interview by author, July 3, 2017.

100. David McReynolds to Bronson Clark, John Collins, Richard Deats, March 9, 1982; David McReynolds to Bronson Clark, Richard Deats, John Collins, Randy Kehler, David Cortright, March 10, 1982, UNSSDII: June 12 NYC: Executive Committee Meetings, Leslie Cagan Papers, TAM #138, Box 10.

101. David McReynolds to Bronson Clark, John Collins, Richard Deats, March 9, 1982; David McReynolds to Bronson Clark, Richard Deats, John Collins, Randy Kehler, David Cortright, March 10, 1982, UNSSDII: June 12 NYC: Executive Committee Meetings, Leslie Cagan Papers, TAM #138, Box 10.

102. Leslie Cagan, interview by author, June 17, 2017.

103. David McReynolds, interview by author, July 3, 2017.

104. Lindorff, "War in Peace," 12.

105. Meyer, *Winter of Discontent*, 186–187.

106. David Cortright, interview by author, March 3, 2017.

107. Flyer, SANE Papers, Series G, Box 67, SCPC.

108. Austin, "10,000 at Interfaith Service Pray for End to Arms Race," 33.

109. Linda Bullard and Mary Noland, letter announcing meeting, May 18, 1982, UNSSDII: Affiliated Activities, United States, Leslie Cagan Papers, TAM #138, Box 10.

110. Kathy Engel, interview by author, July 6, 2017.

111. Leslie Cagan, interview by author, June 1, 2017.

Chapter 4 · June 12, 1982

1. Leslie Cagan, interview by author, June 1, 2017.

2. June 12 Rally Committee Fact Sheet, June 11, 1982; UNSSDII: June 12, NYC: Rally Committee Meetings, Leslie Cagan Papers, TAM #138, Box 10; Montgomery, "Throngs Fill Manhattan," 1; Andersen, White, and Zagorin, "Movement Gathers Force," *Time*, 39, UNSSDII: June 12, NYC: Press Coverage, Leslie Cagan Papers, TAM #138, Box 10; Cortright, *Peace Works*, 5.

3. June 12 Rally Committee Fact Sheet, June 11, 1982; UNSSDII: June 12, NYC: Rally Committee Meetings, Leslie Cagan Papers, TAM #138, Box 10.

4. Andersen, White, and Zagorin, "Movement Gathers Force," 39.

5. June 12 Rally Committee Logistics Fact Sheet, SANE Papers, Series G, Box 67; Anekwe, "Colors Finally Blended in Giant Peace Protest," 1.

6. Leslie Cagan to rally supporters, n.d., UNSSDII: June 12, NYC: Logistics, March Route, Leslie Cagan Papers, TAM #138, Box 10; Warburg and Lowe, *You Can't Hug with Nuclear Arms.*

7. Warburg and Lowe, *You Can't Hug with Nuclear Arms.*

8. Anekwe, "Colors Finally Blended in Giant Peace Protest," 1.

9. Warburg and Lowe, *You Can't Hug with Nuclear Arms*; June 12 Rally Committee Press Release, May 25, 1982, UNSSDII: June 12, NYC: Media Task Force, Press Releases, Leslie Cagan Papers, TAM #138, Box 10.

10. "Summary of Activities on June 12th," n.d. UNSSDII: June 12, NYC: Rally Program, Leslie Cagan Papers, TAM #138, Box 10.

11. "Peace Fronts," *Whole Life Times*, July/August 1982, 18, UNSSDII: June 12, NYC: Press Coverage, Leslie Cagan Papers, TAM #138, Box 10.

12. Warburg and Lowe, *You Can't Hug with Nuclear Arms.*

13. Warburg and Lowe, *You Can't Hug with Nuclear Arms*; Montgomery, "Throngs Fill Manhattan," 1.

14. Summary of Activities on June 12th, n.d. UNSSDII: June 12, NYC: Rally Program, Leslie Cagan Papers, TAM #138, Box 10; Warburg and Lowe, *You Can't Hug with Nuclear Arms.*

15. H. D. Quigg, "700,000 March through Manhattan Calling for End to Nuclear Weapons," *Sunday Star-Bulletin & Advertiser*, June 13, 1982, A-5, UNSSDII: June 12, NYC: Press Coverage, Leslie Cagan Papers, TAM #138, Box 10; Warburg and Lowe, *You Can't Hug with Nuclear Arms*; David Cortright, *Peace Works*, 6; *In Our Hands*, Official Program.

16. Helen Caldicott, interview by author, April 17, 2017; Meyer, *Winter of Discontent*, 129.

17. *In Our Hands*; Meyer, *Winter of Discontent*, 188; "Peace Fronts," *Whole Life Times*, July/August 1982, UNSSDII: June 12, NYC: Press Coverage, Leslie Cagan Papers, TAM #138, Box 10.

18. Montgomery, "Throngs Fill Manhattan," 1; McFadden, "Spectrum of Humanity," 42.

19. Warburg and Lowe, *You Can't Hug with Nuclear Arms.*

20. David McReynolds, interview by author, July 3, 2017.

21. "Peace Fronts," *Whole Life Times*, July/August 1982, 18, UNSSDII: June 12, NYC: Press Coverage, Leslie Cagan Papers, TAM #138, Box 10.

22. Herman, "Children Stage Nuclear Protest," B4; Herman, "Anti-Nuclear Groups Are Using Professions," 26.

23. Herman, "Rally Speakers Decry Cost," 43; Warburg and Lowe, *You Can't Hug with Nuclear Arms.*

24. Andersen, White, and Zagorin, "Movement Gathers Force," 39, UNSSDII: June 12, NYC: Press Coverage, Leslie Cagan Papers, TAM #138, Box 10.

25. Warburg and Lowe, *You Can't Hug with Nuclear Arms.*

26. Seymour Chwast, interview by author, June 26, 2017.

27. Leslie Cagan, interview by author, June 15, 2017.

28. Murray Rosenblith, *Win*, May 15, 1982, 16–17, UNSSDII: Affiliated Activities, United States, Leslie Cagan Papers, TAM #138, Box 10.

29. Anekwe, "Colors Finally Blended in Giant Peace Protest," 1.

30. Anekwe, "Colors Finally Blended in Giant Peace Protest," 1.

31. Anekwe, "Colors Finally Blended in Giant Peace Protest," 1; Herman, "Rally Speakers Decry Cost," 43.

32. Quigg, "700,000 March through Manhattan," A-5.

33. "Resolution on Nuclear Disarmament," *New York Amsterdam News*, June 12, 1982, 33.

34. June 12 Rally Committee Logistics Fact Sheet, SANE Papers, Series G, Box 67; Simon Anekwe, "Nuke Protest," *New York Amsterdam News*, June 12, 1982, 1.

35. National Gay Task Force Press Release, June 23, 1982, UNSSDII: June 12, NYC: Rally Program, Leslie Cagan Papers, TAM #138, Box 10.

36. National Gay Task Force Press Release, June 23, 1982, UNSSDII: June 12, NYC: Rally Program, Leslie Cagan Papers, TAM #138, Box 10.

37. Montgomery, "Throngs Fill Manhattan," 1.

38. Leslie Cagan, interview by author, June 15, 2017.

39. June Action to Leslie Cagan, May 24, 1982, UNSSDII: June 12 NYC: Correspondence, Leslie Cagan Papers, TAM #138, Box 10.

40. Concerned Citizens on Nuclear Arms letter to June 12 Rally Committee, n.d., UNSSDII: Affiliated Activities, United States, Leslie Cagan Papers, TAM #138, Box 10.

41. "Peace Sunday Draws Crowd of 100,000," *Los Angeles Sentinel*, June 10, 1982, A4. LeVar Burton, who played Kunta Kinte in *Roots*, was the keynote speaker at multiple events in July for the California Nuclear Weapons Freeze Campaign. "'Roots' Star Speaks For Nuke Freeze," *Los Angeles Sentinel*, July 8, 1982, C12.

42. "March & Rally For Nuclear Disarmament and Human Needs" flyer, UNSSDII: Affiliated Activities, United States, Leslie Cagan Papers, TAM #138, Box 10; Cortright, *Peace Works*, 7.

43. Warburg and Lowe, *You Can't Hug with Nuclear Arms.*

44. David Cortright interview by author, March 3, 2017.

45. Warburg and Lowe, *You Can't Hug with Nuclear Arms.*

46. Warburg and Lowe, *You Can't Hug with Nuclear Arms.*

47. Cortright, *Peace Works*, 5; Quigg, "700,000 March through Manhattan," A-5; David Cortright, interview by author, March 3, 2017.

48. Warburg and Lowe, *You Can't Hug with Nuclear Arms*.

49. Helen Caldicott, interview by author, April 17, 2017.

50. Warburg and Lowe, *You Can't Hug with Nuclear Arms*.

51. Murray Rosenblith, *Win*, May 15, 1982, 16–17, UNSSDII: Affiliated Activities, United States, Leslie Cagan Papers, TAM #138, Box 10.

52. Rosenblith, *Win*, 16–17.

53. Warburg and Lowe, *You Can't Hug with Nuclear Arms*.

54. Warburg and Lowe, *You Can't Hug with Nuclear Arms*.

Chapter 5 · The Legacy of June 12 and Beyond

1. Richard Hudson in Warburg and Lowe, *You Can't Hug With Nuclear Arms!*

2. Mattern, "Requiem for a Not So Special Session," 58–59.

3. Jaffe, "Why the Second Session Flopped," 174–176.

4. Perlez, "White House Has Little to Say," B6.

5. Daley, "How Reagan Brought the World to the Brink."

6. Maar, *Freeze!*, 3; Cortright, *Peace Works*, 102.

7. Cortright, *Peace Works*, 103.

8. David Cortright, interview by author, March 13, 2017.

9. Cortright, *Peace Works*, 90–91.

10. Daley, "How Reagan Brought the World to the Brink."

11. Daley, "How Reagan Brought the World to the Brink."

12. Cortright, *Peace Works*, 103.

13. Cortright, *Peace Works*, 104–105.

14. Knoblauch, *Nuclear Freeze in a Cold War*, x.

15. Cortright, *Peace Works*, 96.

16. Daley, "Thirty Years Ago Today."

17. Daley, "Thirty Years Ago Today."

18. Cortright, *Peace Works*, 1.

19. Helen Caldicott, interview by author, April 7, 2017.

20. Mike Myerson, interview by author, July 7, 2017.

21. Kathy Engel, interview by author, July 6, 2017.

22. Randy Kehler, interview by author, June 2, 2017.

23. Leslie Cagan, interview by author, June 1, 2017.

24. Michael Krepon, interviewed on *Press the Button* podcast, November 16, 2020. See also Krepon, *Winning and Losing the Nuclear Peace*.

25. Rubinson, *Rethinking the American Antinuclear Movement*, x.

26. United Nations Office of Disarmament Affairs, https://www.un.org/disarmament/wmd/nuclear/tpnw/.

27. Acheson, "New Generation against the Bomb."
28. Acheson, "New Generation against the Bomb."
29. Leslie Cagan, interview by author, June 1, 2017.
30. Leslie Cagan, interview by author, June 1, 2017.
31. David Cortright, interview by author, March 13, 2017.
32. David McReynolds, interview by author, July 3, 2017.
33. Solnit, "Protest and Persist." See also Solnit, *Hope in the Dark*.
34. Kathy Engel, interview by author, July 6, 2017.

Interviews

Krepon, Michael, interview by Michelle Dover and Tom Collina. "Our Common Humanity." Produced by Ploughshares Fund. *Press the Button.* November 17, 2020. Podcast, MP3 audio, 46:16. https://pressthebutton.libsyn. com/our-common-humanity.

Leslie Cagan	Joseph Gerson
Helen Caldicott	Randy Kehler
Seymour Chwast	David McReynolds
David Cortright	Michael Myerson
Kathy Engel	Cora Weiss

Film

Richter, Robert, and Stanley Warnow, dirs. *In Our Hands.* June 12 Film Group, 1984.

Manuscript Sources

American Friends Services Committee Records, Swarthmore College Peace Collection (SCPC)
American Peace Crusade Records, SCPC
American Women for Peace Records, SCPC
Blacks Against Nukes Records, SCPC
Chicago Peace Council Records, SCPC
Coalition for a Non-Nuclear World Records, SCPC
Coalition for a Nuclear Free Harbor Records, SCPC
Coalition for a Nuclear Test Ban Records, SCPC
Coalition for Nuclear Disarmament Records, SCPC
Committee for a Sane Nuclear Policy Records, SCPC
Committee for Non-Violent Action Records, SCPC

Fellowship of Reconciliation (United States) Records, SCPC
Hiroshima-Nagasaki Commemorations Records, SCPC
Hiroshima Peace Center Records, SCPC
Hiroshima Peace Pilgrimage Records, SCPC
Hiroshima Peace Society Records, SCPC
Homer A. Jack Papers, SCPC
Illinois Nuclear Weapons Freeze Campaign Records, SCPC
James Haughton Papers, Schomburg Center for Research in Black Culture
Leslie Cagan Papers, Tamiment Library and Robert F. Wagner Labor Archives,
    New York University
National Campaign for No-First-Use of Nuclear Weapons Records, SCPC
National Committee for Radiation Victims Records, SCPC
National Committee on Atomic Information Records, LOC
Nuclear Weapons Freeze Campaign Records, SCPC
Performing Artists for Nuclear Disarmament Records, SCPC
Riverside Church Disarmament Records, SCPC
War Resisters League Records, SCPC
Women's International League for Peace and Freedom (United States) Records,
    SCPC

Periodicals

Arms Control Today
Bulletin of the Atomic Scientists
Chicago Globe
Chicago Tribune
Detroit Free Press
Fellowship
Gay Community News
Life
Los Angeles Sentinel
Los Angeles Times
The Nation
National Guardian
New York Amsterdam News
New York Herald Tribune
New York Times
Newsweek
Nuclear Times
Philadelphia Tribune
San Francisco Chronicle
Time

USA Today
US News and World Report
Village Voice
Washington Afro-American
Washington Post
WIN
WRL News

Books

Acheson, Ray. *Banning the Bomb, Smashing the Patriarchy*. New York: Rowman and Littlefield, 2021.

Badash, Lawrence. *A Nuclear Winter's Tale: Science and Politics in the 1980s*. Cambridge, MA: MIT Press, 2009.

Bennett, Scott H. *Radical Pacifism: The War Resisters League and Gandhian Nonviolence in America, 1915–1963*. Syracuse, NY: Syracuse University Press, 2003.

Blackwell, Joyce. *No Peace without Freedom: Race and the Women's International League for Peace and Freedom, 1915–1975*. Carbondale: Southern Illinois University Press, 2004.

Caldicott, Helen. *A Desperate Passion: An Autobiography*. New York: W. W. Norton, 1997.

Carter, April. *Peace Movements: International Protest and World Politics since 1945*. London: Routledge, 1992.

Chatfield, Charles. *The American Peace Movement: Ideals and Activism*. New York: Twayne Publishers, 1992.

Colbert, Sonya Diggs. *Radical Vision: A Biography of Lorraine Hansberry*. New Haven, CT: Yale University Press, 2021.

Cole, Paul M., and William J. Taylor, Jr., eds. *The Nuclear Freeze Debate*. Boulder, CO: Westview Press, 1983.

Cortright, David. *Peace Works: The Citizen's Role in Ending the Cold War*. Boulder, CO: Westview Press, 1993.

Foster, Catherine. *Women for All Seasons: The Story of the Women's International League for Peace and Freedom*. Athens: University of Georgia Press, 1989.

Gamson, William A. *The Strategy of Social Protest*. Homewood, IL: Dorsey Press, 1975.

Gerson, Joseph. *Empire and the Bomb: How the US Uses Nuclear Weapons to Dominate the World*. London: Pluto Press, 2007.

Holsworth, Robert D. *Let Your Life Speak: A Study of Politics, Religion, and Antinuclear Weapons Activism*. Madison: University of Wisconsin Press, 1989.

Intondi, Vincent J. *African Americans Against the Bomb: Nuclear Weapons, Colonialism, and the Black Freedom Movement.* Stanford, CA: Stanford University Press, 2015.

Japan Broadcasting Company, ed. *Unforgettable Fire: Pictures Drawn by Atomic Bomb Survivors.* New York: Pantheon Books, 1977.

Jenkins, Philip. *Decade of Nightmares: The End of the Sixties and the Making of Eighties America.* Oxford: Oxford University Press, 2006.

Johnston, Carla B. *Reversing the Nuclear Arms Race.* Cambridge, MA: Schenkman Books, 1986.

Knoblauch, William M. *Nuclear Freeze in a Cold War: The Reagan Administration, Cultural Activism, and the End of the Arms Race.* Amherst: University of Massachusetts Press, 2017.

Kojm, Christopher A., ed. *The Nuclear Freeze Debate.* New York: H. R. Wilson, 1983.

Kozol, Jonathan. *Savage Inequalities: Children in America's Schools.* New York: Harper Perennial, 1991.

Krepon, Michael. *Winning and Losing the Nuclear Peace: The Rise, Demise, and Revival of Arms Control.* Redwood City, CA: Stanford University Press, 2021.

Loeb, Paul Rogat. *Hope in Hard Times: America's Peace Movement and the Reagan Era.* Lexington, MA: Lexington Books, 1987.

Lofland, John. *Polite Protesters: The American Peace Movement of the 1980s.* Syracuse, NY: Syracuse University Press, 1993.

Maar, Henry Richard, III. *Freeze! The Grassroots Movement to Halt the Arms Race and End the Cold War.* Ithaca, NY: Cornell University Press, 2021.

Marable, Manning. *How Capitalism Underdeveloped Black America.* Cambridge, MA: South End Press, 2000.

Markle, Gerald E., and Frances B. McCrea. *Minutes to Midnight: Nuclear Weapons Protest in America.* Newbury Park, CA: Sage, 1989.

Marullo, Sam, and John Lofland, eds. *Peace Action in the Eighties.* New Brunswick, NJ: Rutgers University Press, 1990.

Meyer, David S. *A Winter of Discontent: The Nuclear Freeze and American Politics.* New York: Praeger, 1990.

Miller, Steven E., ed. *The Nuclear Weapons Freeze and Arms Control.* Cambridge, MA: Ballinger, 1984.

Nunez, Ralph da Costa. *A Shelter Is Not a Home . . . Or Is It? Lessons from Family Homelessness in New York City.* New York: White Tiger Press, 2004.

Phillips, Kevin. *The Politics of Rich and Poor: Wealth and the American Electorate in the Reagan Aftermath.* New York: Random House, 1990.

Price, Jerome. *The Antinuclear Movement.* Boston: Twayne Publishers, 1982.

Rubinson, Paul. *Rethinking the American Antinuclear Movement.* New York: Routledge Press, 2018.

Scheer, Robert. *With Enough Shovels: Reagan, Bush, and Nuclear War.* New York: Random House, 1982.

Schell, Jonathan. *The Fate of the Earth.* New York: Alfred A. Knopf, 1982.

———. *The Gift of Time: The Case for Abolishing Nuclear Weapons Now.* New York: Metropolitan Books, 1998.

Schwab, Gabriele. *Radioactive Ghosts.* Minneapolis: University of Minnesota Press, 2020.

Sidel, Ruth. *Keeping Women and Children Last: America's War on the Poor.* New York: Penguin Books, 1996.

Solo, Pam. *From Protest to Policy: Beyond the Freeze to Common Security.* Cambridge, MA: Ballinger, 1988.

Smith, Jackie, Charles Chatfield, and Ron Pagnucco, eds. *Transnational Movements and Global Politics: Solidarity Beyond the State.* Syracuse, NY: Syracuse University Press, 1997.

Smith, Jennifer, ed. *The Antinuclear Movement.* San Diego: Greenhaven Press, 2003.

Solnit, Rebecca. *Hope in the Dark: Untold Histories, Wild Possibilities.* Chicago: Haymarket Books, 2016.

Stassen, Glen Harold, and Lawrence S. Wittner, eds. *Peace Action: Past, Present, and Future.* Boulder, CO: Paradigm Publishers, 2007.

Torr, James D., ed. *Ronald Reagan.* San Diego: Greenhaven Press, 2001.

Vivian, Octavia. *Coretta: The Story of Coretta Scott King.* Minneapolis: Fortress Press, 2006.

Waller, Douglas C. *Congress and the Nuclear Freeze: An Inside Look at the Politics of a Mass Movement.* Amherst: University of Massachusetts Press, 1987.

Warburg, Jennifer, and Doug Lowe, eds. *You Can't Hug with Nuclear Arms: Photos from June 12 and Related Disarmament Demonstrations.* Dobbs Ferry, NY: Morgan and Morgan, 1982.

Wittner, Lawrence S. *Cold War America: From Hiroshima to Watergate.* New York: Praeger Publishers, 1974.

———. *One World or None: A History of the World Nuclear Disarmament Movement through 1953.* Stanford, CA: Stanford University Press, 1993.

———. *Rebels against War: The American Peace Movement, 1933–1983.* Philadelphia: Temple University Press, 1984.

———. *Resisting the Bomb: A History of the World Nuclear Disarmament Movement, 1954–1970.* Stanford, CA: Stanford University Press, 1997.

———. *Toward Nuclear Abolition: A History of the World Nuclear Disarmament Movement, 1971 to the Present.* Stanford, CA: Stanford University Press, 2003.

Zinn, Howard. "Reagan's Economic Policies Favored the Rich." In *Ronald Reagan,* edited by James D. Torr. San Diego: Greenhaven Press, 2001.

Articles

Acheson, Ray. "A New Generation against the Bomb." *The Nation*. April 27, 2018. http://www.thenation.com/article/archive/a-new-generation-against-the -bomb/.

Andersen, Kurt, Jack E. White, and Adam Zagorin, "A Movement Gathers Force." *Time*. June 21, 1982, 39.

Anekwe, Simon. "Anti-Nuclear Rally to Draw Thousands." *New York Times*. May 22, 1982, 4.

―――. "Colors Finally Blended in Giant Peace Protest." *New York Amsterdam News*. June 19, 1982, 1.

Austin, Charles. "10,000 at Interfaith Service Pray for End to Arms Race." *New York Times*. June 12, 1982, 33.

Basler, Barbara. "Park Rally Tomorrow Is Expected to Cause Extensive Tie-Ups." *New York Times*. June 11, 1982, B1.

Blair, William G. "New York City Girds for June 12 Antinuclear Rally." *New York Times*. June 3, 1982, A11.

Butterfield, Fox. "Anatomy of the Nuclear Protest." *New York Times*. July 11, 1982, SM14.

Cockburn, Alexander, and James Ridgeway. "Peace in Central Park." *Village Voice*. June 22, 1982, 21.

Daley, Tad. "How Reagan Brought the World to the Brink of Nuclear Destruction." AlterNet. February 7, 2011. http://www.alternet.org/2011/02/how _reagan_brought_the_world_to_the_brink_of_nuclear_destruction/.

―――. "Thirty Years Ago Today, at the Nuclear Freeze Rally in Central Park, We Saved Ourselves from Ourselves." *Huffpost*. August 12, 2012. http://www .huffingtonpost.com/tad-daley/nuclear-war-protest_b_1588344.html.

De Nitto, Emily. "June 12 Buildup Gaining Support." *Daily World*. April 30, 1982, 2.

Donner, Frank. "But Will They Come? The Campaign to Smear the Nuclear Freeze Movement." *The Nation*. November 6, 1982, 456–465.

Engel, Pamela. "Donald Trump: I Would Bomb the Sh-t Out of ISIS." *Business Insider*. November 13, 2015. https://www.businessinsider.com/donald-trump -bomb-isis-2015-11.

Fairbanks, Amanda M. "Cora Weiss: A Life in Full." *East Hampton Star*. August 18, 2016. http://easthamptonstar.com/Lead-article/2016818/Cora-Weiss -Lif-Full.

Falk, Florence. "Performing-Arts Group for Atom Curb Formed." *New York Times*. April 4, 1982, 55.

Feron, James. "Momentum Gains on Nuclear-Limit Rally." *New York Times*. June 6, 1982, WC1.

Franklin, Ben A. "Diverse Groups Mobilize for a Weekend of Protests in Capital." *New York Times*. April 20, 1985, 7.

Freedman, Rita. "A Nuclear Freeze Imperils Peace." *New York Times*. June 17, 1982, A26.

Gaouette, Nicole, and Barbara Starr. "Facing Growing North Korea Nuke Threat, Trump Vows: 'It Won't Happen.'" CNN. January 3, 2017. https://www.cnn.com/2017/01/02/politics/north-korea-icbm-threat-trump/.

Gerzhoy, Gene, and Nicholas Miller. "Donald Trump Thinks More Countries Should Have Nuclear Weapons." *Washington Post*. August 6, 2016. https://www.washingtonpost.com/news/monkey-cage/wp/2016/04/06/should-more-countries-have-nuclear-weapons-donald-trump-thinks-so/.

Gray, Colin S., and Keith Paine. "Victory Is Possible." *Foreign Policy* no. 39 (Summer 1980): 14–27.

Guttenplan, D. D. "Who Is Jack O'Dell?" *The Nation*. August 11, 2014. https://www.thenation.com/article/archive/who-jack-odell/.

Herman, Robin. "Anti-Nuclear Groups Are Using Professions as Rallying Points." *New York Times*. June 5, 1982, 26.

———. "Children Stage Nuclear Protest in Central Park." *New York Times*. May 17, 1982, B4.

———. "Protesters Old and New Forge Alliance of Antinuclear Rally. *New York Times*. June 4, 1982, 6.

———. "Rally Speakers Decry Cost of Nuclear Arms Race." *New York Times*. June 13, 1982, 43.

Intondi, Vincent J. "The Fight Continues: Reflections on the June 12, 1982 Rally for Nuclear Disarmament." Arms Control Association. June 10, 2018. http://www.armscontrol.org/blog/2018-06-10/fight/continues-reflections-june-12-1982-rally-nuclear-disarmament.

Isaacs, John. "The Freeze." *Bulletin of the Atomic Scientists*. October 1982, 9–11.

Jaffe, Susan. "Performing Artists Rally for a Nuclear Arms Freeze." *Boston Globe*. April 7, 1982, 6.

———. "Why the Second Session Flopped." *The Nation*. September 4, 1982, 174–76.

Kihss, Peter. "50 in Peace Group to Get Visas for Session at U.N." *New York Times*. June 4, 1982, B1, B6.

Lanset, Andy. "WNYC Covers the Great Anti-Nuclear March and Rally at Central Park June 12, 1982." New York Public Radio. June 12, 2015. https://www.wnyc.org/story/wnyc-covers-great-anti-nuclear-march-and-rally-central-park-june-12-1982/.

Lewis, Diane E. "Protesters Link Deaths of Poor to Arms Shift." *Boston Globe*. February 7, 1982, 30.

Lindorff, David. "War in Peace: The Fight for Position in New York's June 12 Disarmament Rally." *Village Voice*. April 20, 1982, 12.

LoBianco, Tom. "Donald Trump on Terrorists: 'Take Out Their Families.'" CNN. December 3, 2015. https://www.cnn.com/2015/12/02/politics/donald-trump-terrorists-families/.

Lueck, Thomas J. "Disarmament Rally Is Biggest Since 1982." *New York Times.* June 12, 1988, 34.

Mattern, Douglas. "Requiem for a Not So Special Session." *Bulletin of the Atomic Scientists.* November, 1982, 58–59.

McFadden, Robert D. "A Spectrum of Humanity Represented at the Rally." *New York Times.* June 13, 1982, 42.

Meisel, Duncan. "The Nuclear Freeze Campaign Prevented an Apocalypse, So Can the Climate Movement." Common Dreams. May 26, 2015. http://www .helencaldicott.com/the-nuclear-freeze-campaign-prevented-an-apocalypse-so -can-the-climate-movement.

Miller, Judith. "3 Women and the Campaign for a Nuclear Freeze." *New York Times.* May 26, 1982. https://www.nytimes.com/1982/05/26/us/3-women-and -the-campaign-for-a-nuclear-freeze.html.

Mincey, Pamela. "Afro-Americans Get Set For June 12." *Daily World.* February 25, 1982, 3.

Montgomery, Paul L. "Throngs Fill Manhattan to Protest Nuclear Weapons." *New York Times.* June 13, 1982. http://www.nytimes.com/1982/06/13/world /throngs-fill-manhattan-to-protest-nuclear-weapon.html.

Mount, Adam. "The Biden Nuclear Posture Review: Obstacles to Reducing Reliance on Nuclear Weapons." *Arms Control Today* 52, no. 1 (January/ February 2022): 7.

Nichols, Tom. "I Want My Mutually Assured Destruction: How 1980s MTV Helped My Students Understand the Cold War." *Atlantic.* May 8, 2021. http://www.theatlantic.com/ideas/archive/2021/05/my-mtv-cold-war -retrospective/618812/.

"Peace Sunday Draws Crowd of 100,000." *Los Angeles Sentinel.* June 10, 1982, A4.

Perlez, Jane. "White House Has Little to Say on Atom Protest." *New York Times.* June 14, 1982, B6.

Quigg, H. D. "700,000 March through Manhattan Calling for End to Nuclear Weapons." *Sunday Star-Bulletin and Advertiser.* June 13, 1982, A-5.

Richardson, David B. "On the March—U.S. Version of Peace Crusade." *US News and World Report.* March 22, 1982, 24–26.

Sobran, Joseph "Rainbow in Central Park." *National Review.* July 9, 1982, 32–34.

Solnit, Rebecca. "Protest and Persist: Why Giving Up Hope is Not an Option." *The Guardian.* March 13, 2017. https://www.theguardian.com/world/2017 /mar/13/protest-persist-hope-trump-activism-anti-nuclear-movement.

Schell, Jonathan. "The Spirit of June 12." *The Nation.* June 14, 2007. http://www .thenation.com/Article/spirit-june-12/.

Sweet, William. "Reflections on 30th Anniversary of June 12 Peace Rally." *Foreign Policy Association.* June 16, 2012. http://foreignpolicyblogs.com/2012 /06/16/reflections-30th-anniversary-of-june-12-peace-rally/.

Tilchen, Maida. "Lesbians, Gays and the UN Disarmament March." *Gay Community News.* March 20, 1982, 3.

Trinkl, John. "Giant Disarmament Rally Planned for June." *Guardian.* February 10, 1982, 6.

——. "Plans Build for Disarmament Rally June 12." *Guardian.* May 5, 1982, 2–3.

Wittner, Lawrence. "The Forgotten Years of the World Nuclear Disarmament Movement, 1975–1978." *Journal of Peace Research* 40, no. 4 (July 2003): 435–456.